THE TWELVE STEPS
in the Bible

A Path to Wholeness for Adult Children

by Michele S. Matto

PAULIST PRESS
New York, Mahwah, N.J.

Acknowledgements

THE TWELVE STEPS OF ALCOHOLICS ANONYMOUS

1. We admitted we were powerless over alcohol— that our lives had become unmanageable. 2. Came to believe that a Power greater than ourselves could restore us to sanity. 3. Made a decision to turn our will and our lives over to the care of God as we understood Him. 4. Made a searching and fearless moral inventory of ourselves. 5. Admitted to God, to ourselves and to another human being the exact nature of our wrongs. 6. Were entirely ready to have God remove all these defects of character. 7. Humbly asked Him to remove our shortcomings. 8. Made a list of all persons we had harmed, and became willing to make amends to them all. 9. Made direct amends to such people wherever possible, except when to do so would injure them or others. 10. Continued to take personal inventory and when we were wrong promptly admitted it. 11. Sought through prayer and meditation to improve our conscious contact with God, praying only for knowledge of His will for us and the power to carry that out. 12. Having had a spiritual awakening as the result of these steps, we tried to carry this message to alcoholics, and to practice these principles in all our affairs.

The Twelve Steps are reprinted and adapted with permission of Alcoholics Anonymous World Services, Inc. Permission to reprint and adapt the Twelve Steps does not mean that AA has reviewed or approved the content of this publication, nor that AA agrees with the views expressed herein. AA is a program of recovery from alcoholism. Use of the Twelve Steps in connection with programs and activities which are patterned after AA but which address other problems does not imply otherwise.

Quotations or paraphrases from HOMILY SERVICE, copyright © The Liturgical Conference, 1017 Twelfth Street, Washington, D.C., 20005-4091 are made with the kind permission of the Liturgical Conference. All rights reserved.

"Come to the Water," by John Foley, S.J., copyright © 1978 by John B. Foley, S.J., and New Dawn Music, P.O. Box 13248, Portland, OR 97213-0248. All rights reserved. Used with permission.

Stanza 6 of "Where Charity and Love Prevail," copyright © 1961 by World Library Publications, Inc., is used with permission.

The lyrics for the songs "Dance with Me," "Twilight Journey" and "Solitudes" are reprinted by permission of the songwriter, Robert Baker.

Library of Congress Cataloging-in-Publication Data

Matto, Michele S., 1945–
    The twelve steps in the Bible: a path to wholeness for adult children/ by Michele S. Matto.
      p. cm.
    Includes bibliographical references.
    ISBN 0-8091-3264-8
    1. Adult children of alcoholics—Prayer-books and devotions—English. 2. Twelve-step programs—Religious aspects—Christianity—Meditations. I. Title.
    BV4596.A27M285 1991
    242'.4—dc20   91-24872
                                                    CIP

Published by Paulist Press
997 Macarthur Boulevard
Mahwah, NJ 07430

Printed and bound in the
United States of America

Contents

The Twelve Steps
of Alcoholics Anonymous
adapted for use by Adult Children of Alcoholics

1. We admit that we are powerless over people, places, and circumstances, that our lives have become unmanageable.

2. We come to believe that a power greater than ourselves can restore us to healthy patterns of living and responding.

3. We make a decision to turn our will and our lives over to the care of God as we understand God.

4. We make a searching and fearless moral inventory of ourselves.

5. We admit to God, to ourselves, and to another human being the exact nature of our wrongs.

6. We are entirely ready to have God remove all these defects of character.

7. We humbly ask God to remove our shortcomings.

8. We make a list of all persons we have harmed, and become willing to make amends to them all.

9. We make direct amends to such people wherever possible, except when to do so would injure them or others.

10. We continue to take personal inventory and, when we are wrong, promptly admit it.

11. We seek through prayer and meditation to improve our conscious contact with God, as we understand God, praying only for knowledge of God's will for us and the power to carry that out.

12. Having had a spiritual awakening as the result of these steps, we try to carry this message to others, and to practice these principles in all our affairs.

Introduction

The idea for this Twelve Step approach to the scriptures evolved out of my own participation, during seminary, in Twelve Step meetings for Adult Children of Alcoholics (ACOAs). At such meetings I heard articulated around the discussion circle precisely the kind of faith that, at seminary, we were identifying as true faith: the willingness to walk into the darkness, leaving home and country behind, for the uncertainties that lay ahead, relying on God alone.

But at these meetings I also heard these same people of faith defining themselves as "atheists." The groups were composed largely of people who had left the church and who no longer "believed in God" but rather in their "higher power." Because I bring a Christian orientation to my hearing of their stories, I could only sense that it wasn't God they no longer believed in, but the "God" of their childhood, some cosmic dysfunctional Parent in the sky who was judgmental, punitive, and very conditional and withholding of love. It was not the God of grace revealed in Jesus' life, ministry, death, and resurrection that they had turned from, but the *representation of* that God in their early authority figures—what Ana-Maria Rizzuto calls, in her book *The Birth of the Living God,* their "God representations."

The real God of grace was alive and well and present in these very meetings, accepting and loving them *in* their anger toward their early church experiences or whatever else had pushed them away. Now, with no theological or spiritual direction, but still hungry for the real God, they were blowing around in the spiritual winds without any "ballast," and I saw mirrored in their journeys my own journey that had led me to attend seminary.

In reading the work of Thomas Merton and James Finley's *Palace of Nowhere* about Merton's work, I observed, again and again, language about prayer as the movement from the false self to the true self. At the same time, the ACOA and co-dependency litera-

1

ture (Charles Whitfield, Robert Subby) spoke of co-dependency as an expression of our false self and "recovery" as the movement to the authentic self. Near the end of my time at seminary, I began to be able to integrate these different terminologies and approaches to the spiritual journey—the church's tradition in spiritual direction and the co-dependency recovery literature's approach—and see the common thread that drew them together. The common thread was the Twelve Steps, which are actually the "steps" along the spiritual journey throughout the ages but which, for people alienated from the church and the scriptures, help to "order" the hearing of the word. The Twelve Steps make it clear, for instance, that we don't presume to "make disciples of all nations" until we have first acknowledged our own powerlessness and turned our own lives over to the care of God. First things first—though recognizing that the journey is always a *process* of being and becoming.

In addition to needing a sense of order, ACOAs need to hear *grace* in the scriptures, that is, we need to hear preaching in the indicative rather than in the imperative mode. We need to hear what *God* has done and is doing in our lives rather than what *we* must do better. Because ACOAs have already introjected a great deal of guilt and shame and judge ourselves very harshly, we need to discover the God of grace who picks us up, dusts us off, and shows us new ways of being in the world. In short, ACOAs need to learn to *receive.*

I took these observations to Bishop Edsel Ammons, under whose authority I serve in the West Ohio Conference of the United Methodist Church, and was affirmed in my perceptions of what is needed in the church in order to serve people from dysfunctional families. On November 22, 1987, Christ the King Sunday, we held our first worship service and the Twelve Step ministry was established at Epworth United Methodist Church. Originally intended to address the needs of ACOAs, we soon discovered that the Twelve Step approach we take to the scriptures and Christian community also spoke to people in Overeaters Anonymous, Sex and Love Addicts Anonymous, and Co-dependents Anonymous programs. At present, the ministry is characterized as a ministry to co-dependents. We are not an "anonymous" fellowship, but a United Methodist Church which takes a twelve-step approach to spirituality and the scriptures.

At Epworth Twelve Steps, U.M.C., we avoid parental imagery for God and use the Inclusive Language (RSV) Lectionary. We operate with a minimum of organizational structure, and community evolves out of the worship experience itself rather than from scheduled events, though we do have weekly, non-liturgical, support groups as well: co-dependency discussion groups and groups which gather, for example, to view the current John Bradshaw video series "On the Family."

The reflections in this collection are actually homilies preached at Epworth Twelve Steps United Methodist Church, and are based on the hermeneutics of grace as taught to me by the Reverend Van Bogard Dunn, now retired dean and professor of New Testament at the Methodist Theological School in Ohio, at Delaware. It is a hermeneutic that sees scripture as always *descriptive* rather than *prescriptive* of the Christian life. This is the grace that ACOAs missed somehow in their early religious environments, and largely why they leave the church.

I am grateful to the Liturgical Conference for permission to reproduce these selected exegetical understandings and illustrations from *Homily Service*. They kept me from having to "reinvent the wheel." I appreciate the *Homily Service* in sermon preparation not only for time-efficiency, but also because its use demonstrates that "traditional church" homiletical resources, when carefully and graciously written, *can* be heard by people who have left the institutional church.

I wish to express my gratitude to the Rev. "Bogie" Dunn for the scriptural and spiritual wisdom he has provided along the way, to the Rev. Jeffery Hopper for the Jungian work we did together for four years, out of which came my internalized understandings of the individuation process, and to my bishop, Edsel Ammons, who trusted me with this ministry *before* I had demonstrated "competence." *That* has been, for me, the gospel.

Finally, I wish to thank the people of Epworth Twelve Steps United Methodist Church, and specifically Barbara and Grey Austin, Linda Carter, and Ernesto Vasquez, for their time, effort and expertise in editing, typing, and generally overseeing the preparation of this manuscript.

My family, Ed, Holly, E.J., Kevin, and Aaron, have provided the stuff of life from which all these reflections are drawn. Their questions, support, and encouragement all along the way have sustained me in the hard times. To them I am grateful.

Michele S. Matto
Pentecost 1991

STEP 1

We admit that we are powerless over people, places and circumstances, that our lives have become unmanageable.

Come Dance with Me

Read and reflect: 1 Thessalonians 5:16–24

Many of us have a hard time with these words from Paul. I think it is because, out of our ACOA backgrounds, we tend to hear these kinds of passages as *pre*scriptive rather than *de*scriptive of the spiritual life. That is, we hear them as one more thing we have to *do*—or haven't *done*—rather than as God's invitation to simply "Come dance with me!"

So, I want to explain what, to the best of my understanding, Paul means in this text. The three "themes" of this scripture passage are joy, prayer, and thanksgiving, and they are really not three separate things. Joy and thanksgiving are the bookends around prayer.

To understand the message of grace in this passage, like understanding the message of grace in scripture in general, requires a different way of seeing, which is what the realm of God is actually about, a different way of seeing. In this short passage of Paul's, we find grace in the scriptures, for grace is who God *is* in God's very essence, and for sure what scripture intends to convey.

Paul has been speaking here about our sanctification, which is a word for our growth toward union with God. The key to this whole passage in Paul's letter is tacked on at the very end: "God, who calls you, is faithful, and will do it." That means the whole area of our spiritual growth and life—our journey—is not something we really have to "do." That is why in the Twelve Step program we begin by admitting the fact that we can't do it! We are powerless to do it. That is the first step.

This is a paradox because it is also not the case that we sit on our hands, waiting for life to happen to us. When the steps are begun, God is really in charge, and, like a pregnancy, everything just begins to evolve and grow, kind of on its own—though this is not to say that the mother doesn't need food and vitamins along the way, and at least a midwife at the birthing.

7

So, as we begin to see the journey in the indicative mode, what does it mean to "Rejoice always, pray constantly, and give thanks in all circumstances"?

To begin with, we have to ask: "What is prayer?" When I started seminary, I thought "prayer" would mean getting as deep as possible into the scriptures, and it is certainly true that learning the original Greek text or studying the work of biblical scholars helps us to find grace. But my encounters with learned people have also taught me that you can know the scriptures backward, forward, and upside down, and still minister death.

In one of our seminary courses, we read a book called *Shantung Compound,* about a civilian internment camp in North China during its war with Japan. The prisoners in the camp represented a cross-section of humanity—teachers, businessmen and women, lawyers, doctors, children. The camp became a living laboratory, a miniature society that illustrated the human condition. And the only people out of this very diverse group who did not sell themselves out, who held up when the going got tough, were some monks who were also detained there in the camp. However, the holiness of these monks went completely contrary to everything I had ever been taught about what holiness was. They smuggled in food for the people, stole supplies needed for the sick, and cleaned the latrines when no one else in the camp would stoop to such a task. My reading about these concentration camp experiences taught me what it meant to be a person of prayer. To be a person of prayer came to have a strange new meaning.

As I read more books on prayer, the exciting thing I found was precisely what Paul is saying in this passage: prayer is not what we *do* or one more thing we have to *get right;* it is what God does in us, simply out of our own need and powerlessness. Listen to this quote from one of the classic writers on prayer:

> Helplessness is the real secret and the impelling power of prayer. It is one of the greatest gifts which God can impart to us, for it is only when we are helpless that we open our hearts to God and let God help us in our distress, according to God's grace and mercy.[1]

In the Twelve Step program, prayer is our acknowledgement that we are powerless over our past and that our lives have become unmanageable. That is the basis not only of the Twelve Step program, but of the life of prayer as well. So, when Paul says, "Pray constantly," he doesn't mean "Get on your knees and say some words every five minutes," but he means "Keep always in your mind your innate helplessness and powerlessness." That is prayer, because that acknowledgment opens us to God. St. Augustine said, "Your desire itself is your prayer, and if your desire is continuous, so is your prayer."

We who are in Twelve Step programs are a group of people who have already been brought to our knees by life's circumstances, and who are truly motivated to begin the deepening life of prayer. The Twelve Steps are nothing more and nothing less than what the church has been about all these centuries. Taken seriously, the steps are the crux of the life of prayer. ACOAs are, just in the very fact of having already committed to this program, true seekers on the journey—already people of prayer.

We have simply heard the message backward all these years. When Paul admonishes us in this passage to "keep away from evil," he does not mean, as we ACOAs tend to hear, "Don't make any mistakes; don't screw up." To keep away from evil means exactly the opposite. Evil is the desire to *be* God, infinite, infallible, all-powerful; evil denies our finitude. Evil does not ever *need* any help, thank you. Evil never makes mistakes and knows nothing about powerlessness. To keep away from evil is to *admit* powerlessness and to ask for help in our finite helplessness.

So where, in our everyday lives, do we see anyone "praying constantly"? I mean, out on the sidewalk, where we all live? I remember reading a newspaper article about a woman whose car was hit by a train. The woman flew through the windshield and landed on the pavement. Rescue workers had covered her with a blanket to keep her warm, but she was worried that she might smother. So a bystander, the mother of the children who were playing in the yard where the car landed, crawled under the blanket with her and put it over both of them so she could talk with the injured woman. That was her prayer. "There are moments when, whatever the attitude of the body, the soul is on its knees" (Victor Hugo).

Prayer isn't something we are supposed to do, or something someone decided we should do. Prayer is who we *are,* in God, at the core of our deepest selves. And whenever we are in touch with helplessness, our own or another's, we are somehow connected to each other in prayer. "Emmanuel," which we sing about in the Advent hymn, "O Come, O Come, Emmanuel," means "God with us." God gets under the covers with us so we can talk together when we're hurting. It is this God-with-us who disperses the gloomy clouds of night and puts to flight death's dark shadows.

The *incarnation* is the coming of God to earth in very human form. "Authentic prayer incarnates the sacred in very human forms, and is fundamentally *relationship* in honesty and truth."[2] When our relationship begins to be less than honest, whether with God or with each other, we experience pain, which can be mental, and sometimes physical, but which is always felt at the spiritual level. It is very hard to rejoice and be thankful when we are in pain. But it is a fact, as we in the Twelve Step program know, that pain has a way of motivating us to return to the honesty with self and God and others that forms the life of prayer. For that we can rejoice and be thankful in all things—once we begin to see "pain" in this new way. Many of us have experienced the healing of broken relationships that have gotten real only when one of the people in the relationship was seriously ill and finally there was the pressure to admit the anger that had lain dormant and unexpressed, under the cold blanket of past experiences that were never talked through to resolution.

For many years we thought, or were taught, that holiness precluded anger, but the learning to own and express anger is a crucial part of the life of prayer. Anger is a God-given emotion, and the fact that God stirs that up in us at some point in our recovery is God's voice calling to us to be real—to come out and dance with God *just as we are.*

Prayer is a dance with the one who knows us and calls us by name. To be a partner in the dance does not mean we will not hurt or be sick in this life. It does mean that we have a partner in the dance who wills us to live and be free—who, no matter what our past, has never left us.

In prayer we sing, with Mary, the Magnificat: "Our soul magnifies God and our spirits rejoice in God our savior. For God has taken notice of our condition, and God's mercy goes on from generation to generation, to all who reverence God."

We have a God who dances in the garden's sweet breeze and whose prayer calls to us, "Come out and play with me! Come out and dance with me!"

DANCE WITH ME
(Improvisation on the Lord's Prayer)
by Robert Baker

Sun rises brave, makes a new day.
I rise up and go to the window—
Shake off the night. The Light flows like wine,
    the warm sun caresses my sleepy soul.
O God, I see You there, holding the world in embrace;
And, O God, I hear Your prayer, my life is Your holy place.
O give us this day and open our souls to let in the touch of
    Your happiness.
Teach us Your name, from Love it is made, and we are Your
    children of innocence.
And, O God, I love this world; help me live brave and true.
And, O God, You've never left, and each place I look, there's
    You!
Oh, help us forgive the harms we have caused; we truly know
    not what we do.
Healing is ours to give or withhold; we ask for this power
    from You.
And, O God, I see You here, Your will is to love and be free.
Oh, God, I hear your prayer, is that Your voice calling me?
Oh, yesterday's gone—fades with the dawn, the wounds will
    grow over with tougher skin.
Tomorrow will arrive in its own time; remind us that NOW is
    eternity!
And oh, God, is that You there, dancing in the garden's sweet
    breeze?
Is that Your prayer calling me, "Come out and play with
    Me! . . . Come out and dance with Me!"

Suggestions for Prayer or Journaling:

1. Close your eyes and allow the image of someone you experience
   as a holy person to come before you. What is he or she like? How
   do you experience their "praying constantly"?

2. Reflect back to a time in your life when God was clearly speaking
   to you (or others) *through* your anger. What was the outcome?
   What are your feelings now about this experience?

Crying in the Wilderness

Read and reflect: Luke 3:1–6

The first half of this gospel text jogged my memory about why it took me so long to get interested in the Bible. There were all these people and places I couldn't pronounce or relate to. I never could make any sense out of the things I read in there, so I never really opened it. Bibles collected on my shelf one next to another as occasions came along for which people thought a Bible would be an appropriate gift.

One time, when I was seventeen and my parents were getting divorced and everything in my world seemed to be falling apart, I opened one of them—this big fifteen-pound thing my dad had bought one night from a door-to-door salesman—and I flipped it open to one of these name-and-place registers and tried to find some meaning for my life somewhere there, but to no avail. My parents came into the room where I was, storming at each other, and I shut the book and said to myself, "So much for that!" I never opened the Bible again for another seventeen years. But if I had sought out someone to guide me, here is some of the meaning that would have been available to one crying in the wilderness:

The listing of names in the first half of the text is to say: What follows here is not some "once-upon-a-time" fairy tale. It took place in real people's lives in our history and, to be specific, the year was about 26 or 27 A.D., the fifteenth year of the reign of Tiberius Caesar. If we wanted to talk fifty years from now about the cleanup at the Fernald nuclear plant in Cincinnati, we might put it in historical context by saying: "When Ronald Reagan was president and Dick Celeste was governor of Ohio, John Glenn was senator and Thomas Luken was the representative in Cincinnati . . ." The detailing of who-was-who-when first of all pinpoints the action being described at a specific time in real—our—history.

The second thing that detailing does in this gospel account is to

12

set the activity of John the Baptist over against the power and authority of the political and economic powers of the day. Tiberius Caesar was the stepson of Augustus Caesar and had a lifetime's experience of government by the time he took over at Augustus' death. He brought no new policies and gradually, during twenty-three years of ruling, lost the confidence of the empire. As Jesus' life proceeds in the gospels, whenever we hear "Caesar" mentioned by itself, it is to Tiberius Caesar that reference is being made.

A tetrarch was a ruler of a minor political unit. Annas and his son-in-law Caiaphas (Jn 18:13) controlled the Jewish temple and priests; Caiaphas was the high priest.

So we have all the powerful people located in each of their respective places of worldly and churchly authority. And then the text says, amidst all this, that "the word of God came to John in the wilderness." That is, Luke contrasts the powers of people with the authority of the word of God (1 Cor 1:26–31). Real authority, God's message, comes to this strange man, John the Baptist. This man John was a weird bird by anybody's book. Matthew's account (Mt 3:1–12) tells us that he wore a garment of camel's hair and a leather girdle around his waist, and he ate locusts and wild honey. I think that was a little weird even in biblical times! And it is to this strange man in the wilderness that the word of God comes. It is in the wilderness that John sees salvation up ahead.

It makes a body want to know where is the "wilderness." Where, in our lives, is the place where we can, like John, hear the word of God saying to us that the mountains will be leveled and the crooked paths will be made straight?

When you go back to the original Greek text and look at the word translated here as "wilderness," you find the Greek word *eremos* which means lonely, deserted, uninhabited, or desolate. So, moving beyond the literal meaning for wilderness, the text is telling us that it is precisely in the lonely, desolate, deserted times of our lives that the word of God will come to us. It is precisely our crying in the wilderness that opens us up to the reality that we are not God.

Children know this innately; we all knew it as children, but somewhere along the way it got driven out of us, and often, I think, not just by the dysfunctional family but by a dysfunctional society. Every year my son Aaron sings this little Christmas song that's been floating around for generations: "You'd better watch out, you'd better not cry, you'd better not pout, I'm tellin' you why: Santa

Claus is comin' to town. . . ." One day last Christmas he came to me
before school and said, "You know, I think they just put that part
about not crying in there to make it rhyme, because that doesn't
make any sense—that you can't cry." Out of the mouths of
babes . . . The next day a newsletter came home from his school
validating Aaron's own perceptions about the song.

This text reminds us that it is precisely in the wilderness that we
are called to prepare the way of the Lord. "It is in the uncertain and
ambiguous (occasions), in the (turmoils and) tensions of daily
life . . . the wilderness of personal turmoil—doubt, vocational un-
certainty or transition, grief, fear (or abiding) sorrow . . . marital
tension or estrangement within the family"—it is in these wilderness places that we are called to prepare the way of the Lord.[3]

The text challenges us to look at the places in our lives where
there are "valleys of doubt that need to be lifted up, or mountains of
resentment and prejudice that need to be brought low." It asks us to
examine how our ways of responding to others are not healthy,
either for them or for us?[4]

The call to repentance which John preaches is not a call to a
"worm" theology that says, "I'm a creep! I'm a creep!" That's how
many of us have understood "repentance," but actually the word in
Greek, *metanoia,* means to turn around, to change directions; it is
to alter our patterns of life and behavior. As one author put it, "The
call to repentance is walking through a snowy wood and once again
chancing on the road not taken, but this time having the opportunity to redo our steps." It is a second chance to take the road less
traveled. Advent is this time. It calls us to reflect on our lives and
how we might change while there is yet time.

I would like to share with you a couple of actual wilderness
experiences I had, and what they taught me. While vacationing with
my family in Japan we heard that a ninety-three year old woman
had climbed Mount Fuji, and we decided we'd like to do that before
we left. We packed the things we thought we'd need: water, rain-
coats, snacks, warm changes of clothes and all that, and began.

It's a seven-hour walk up, and four hours back down. Even
though we stayed all night in a cabin to break up the climb, there
were several times when I was concerned we had made a mistake
attempting this trek, given our lack of conditioning and preparation. I had never given the physical exertion a second thought, as-
suming we were all healthy and strong. But when we got up to the

level of the clouds and the air got thinner, and it was cold and raining, so dense and foggy you couldn't see three feet in front of you, I felt really helpless and vulnerable. We turned in for some food and rest, and the next morning we rose at 3 A.M. to watch the sun coming up from near the top of the mountain. It was beautiful. But then again at the last portion of the walk, people were lying on the ground writhing in pain, holding their chests, and the huts were selling cans of oxygen, and when I saw our ten year old son's lips turning blue, I felt such a sense of helplessness. The time to turn around had already passed us by. Truly, this was the wilderness. We were out of reach of medical help, and now, by the time we perceived the reality of the top of Mount Fuji, there was no longer the opportunity to turn back. We were already in it.

The wilderness experience helped me to see with new eyes, once again, that I am not God. My "salvation"—wholeness, help, new life, however you understand that word today—will come from outside myself. And there is not just one wilderness experience, after which we have it all "together." Life is a series of them.

When we came down the mountain and returned to Tokyo, we were wiped out, and as we started to board the train at Shinjuku station, we got separated from our ten year old son Kevin. The doors closed abruptly after he boarded, but before we could board, and the train pulled away for Takadanababa, another major transfer point. Tokyo is a city of twelve million people, and no one speaks English. If I'd ever entertained the idea that you could find a friendly helpful policeman on the platform if you got lost, that fantasy evaporated five weeks before, on the day we arrived. On other day trips I had given the kids a piece of paper to carry which had our apartment address in Japanese so they could always get home, but on the mountain our clothes had all been soaked and we weren't too organized anymore. Truly, this was still—or again—the wilderness.

My husband and I boarded the next train at the same car spot, praying that if Kevin remembered where to get off and if we got off at the same car's place, maybe he would be nearby. That train ride was a long forty days in the wilderness, I can tell you! When we arrived there was Kevin, standing talking with another passenger, the only stranger we met in five weeks who spoke English! This kind of salvation from above is the very thing that Luke is describing in today's gospel text. The spiritual life, like the top of Mount Fuji, is very appealing from the postcards and from afar. But navigating it is not always like the pictures we see. There's a lot that the view from the flowered fields below does not reveal. "We are not called to prepare the way of the Lord from a plateau of perfection or the luxurious vantage point of a mountain peak whose perspective and distance all seems clear and orderly." It is in the desolate and lonely spaces, the scary places of our lives, that the way of the Lord is prepared. That's the way it was in John's day and that's the way it is for us. Nothing changes except the names and places.

As I was finishing this reflection, my secretary came in and told me the school nurse was on the phone and Aaron, our six year old, had a fever and headache and needed to be picked up—probably strep again. Aaron hates strep, and he hates the test and the injection for it even more, so he was crying on the phone, dreading the trip to the doctor who puts a stick down his throat and a needle into his bottom whether he consents or not.

When I got to school, his teacher was holding him in her lap and stroking his forehead, as he cried softly. I took him to get some children's Tylenol, and there at the pharmacy Johnny Mathis was singing again, "You'd better watch out, you'd better not cry . . ." We tried to ignore it, and I brought him home and put him to bed with his blue bear and some psalms I've sung and put on tape for him. The first one on the tape, Psalm 131, is my own favorite, which I begin each day with, "Come to the Quiet": "Come and still your soul, like a child at rest on its daddy's knee. . . . Come and still your soul completely, in the quiet."

And I thought to myself, as I watched Aaron relax and fall asleep, "Truly, it is our crying in the wilderness that prepares the way of the Lord."

Suggestions for Prayer or Journaling:

1. How is the admission of your own powerlessness over people, places and circumstances like a wilderness for you?

2. Where is the scary or lonely place in your life right now where you discern God speaking to you? What is God saying?

3. Listen to John Michael Talbot's album "Come to the Quiet," or read Psalm 131.

STEP 2

**We come to believe that a power greater than
ourselves can restore us to healthy patterns of
living and responding.**

Grace: A Power Greater Than Ourselves

Read and reflect: 1 Corinthians 1:3–9

When we read Paul's words at the beginning of 1 Corinthians —"Grace to you, and peace, from God . . ."—we often tend to treat them as simply a greeting and move on to seek whatever the "real" message is going to be. A few weeks ago when Ron (my pastoral colleague) and I looked at the Advent and Christmas texts, pondering what and how to preach on them, he said, "Look at this; there's the whole sermon: 'Grace to you and peace from God . . .' " And with a laugh and no further discussion necessary, we both understood the point.

The spiritual life begins with a sense of what "grace" is; for grace is who God is in God's very essence. Grace is a power that brings us to our knees in the most sublime and positive sense of that experience. It comes absolutely free to us, undeserved and unearned. It seems to drop down upon us in the most unexpected ways and at the most unexpected times.

Grace comes to us where we are and loves us unconditionally as we are, and it is in that love that we experience the power of God, which is greater than ourselves, to restore us. In the Twelve Step program, we call this the second step. In the Greek New Testament, this power of God is expressed by the word *dynamis,* from which we get our word for "dynamite"—*that* kind of power!

It is difficult to articulate this relationship between grace and power, because we experience it so individually, so uniquely. Perhaps sharing some real-life experiences will be illuminating.

Prayer is letting the real emerge, and that happens most often, it seems, through accepting our woundedness. Last spring a woman at an ACOA meeting spoke of her feelings of being overwhelmed when her parents died within a month of each other. She said, "It

19

has brought a lot of humility into my life because I had to start being real in front of a lot of people I hadn't been. One day I just cried in front of my English class. Somehow in all that, I realized that I don't have to do everything myself. I turned it over to my higher power and said, 'You figure it out; I just can't do it anymore.' That afternoon the doorbell rang and two fifteen year olds were on my step offering to help me with my grading of papers. They have been helping me all year, and it has really helped lighten the grieving process for me."

"Grace to you, and peace, from God."

In the process of writing a book on the spiritual needs of adult children of alcoholics, I distributed a questionnaire to a group of ACOAs. Tears came to my eyes when I read of one woman's grandmother-God figure, whose name was Grace. It brought back memories of my own great-grandmother who, when I stayed overnight at her house, would fix me soft-boiled eggs in the morning—my favorite. She stood hunched over the kitchen sink with her gnarled arthritic hands, digging the eggs out from their hot shells. I remember feeling guilty (of course!) as I watched her, and even telling her, "You don't have to do that, Grandma." She would just keep working, laughing her smiling, twinkly-eyed, gold-toothed laugh that said, "Oh, child!" No words, no lectures, no explanations. Just soft-boiled eggs warm in my bowl. And when I dropped crumbs on the floor from the toast—the one thing she asked me to try not to do, because of the ants, but which I always somehow seemed to do—she just got a rag and cleaned up the crumbs. No judgment, no moralism, no words. Just Grace. But her name was Anna, and I was thirty-six years old and in seminary before I realized that her name was . . . Grace.

"Grace to you, and peace, from God."

When I first attended seminary one professor and I were, for some time, definitely not "in communion." His manner of teaching the gospels was very harsh, and I became confused by the mixed messages I experienced in his class.

He locked us out if we were late to class, and he would not let us tape his lectures because he said he did not trust us not to edit them in ways that would make him look foolish. He placed those of us who had not yet taken Greek in a study group called "*Skotos*" which means darkness, and he hit the slide screen so hard with his pointer that we jumped out of our seats. One man who had been in

Vietnam dropped the class because he started having flashbacks in which his sergeant appeared. I remained, but sat with my book closed and responded "I don't know" to everything he ever asked me. I totally froze him out. When my pastor told me he ran into him at the barber shop and that the professor expressed sadness over our relationship, I replied, "We don't *have* a relationship."

One day in chapel, I was returning from the communion table where I had experienced real power in the eucharist. I don't understand how that happens—no one does—but it is a very humbling experience. You can recognize it by those feelings of having been humbled, feelings that come only from God's powerful presence in grace.

As I returned to my place, I looked down, and this very person had been sitting right under my nose. I put my hand on his shoulder and said, "I am sorry about our broken relationship, and I apologize for *my* part in that." He put his hand on mine, absolutely flabbergasted. He couldn't even speak. He stammered something, and we were both really taken by surprise.

That is the power of Christ in the eucharist. It is not I myself, or you yourself, who ever does those things. We are too proud and arrogant to ever stoop to an apology that the other does not "deserve." I know *I* am anyway!

But *this* is a power *greater* than ourselves. The next year this man died an agonizing death, and I was glad that he and I had come into communion one with another before his death.

"Grace to you, and peace, from God."

Last year when I was processing a lot of these understandings about the relationship between grace and power, I had a dream the night before I left for a trip to Vermont. At the time, the dream made no sense to me. It was about a three or four foot sculpture, a white, unpainted mock-up of Michelangelo's Sistine Chapel, which I was looking at and considering buying at this art sale. I was very intrigued because it was all white and as yet unpainted, and I thought, "*This* is the way Michelangelo would have seen the Sistine Chapel, not the way *we* see it." The price seemed reasonable, so I decided to buy it.

I shared the dream the next morning with my companion on this journey, but we had other more important things to talk about, and it slipped between the cracks. Driving in the car then, I put on a tape I had just received of Father Leo Booth, an English priest, speaking on the subject of "Spirituality and ACOAs." Father Booth concluded his talk in this way:

> You remember the movie ET? You all saw ET? When they were advertising ET, in all the advertisements they showed the finger of ET reaching out for the finger of the little boy. But that wasn't Stephen Spielberg; that goes right back to another great creative man, Michelangelo. High on the Sistine Chapel is the finger of Adam reaching to the finger of God. The image: the power has been given. We have been given it all; all we need to do is reach for it. ACOAs, we can do what we want to do! All we've got to do is decide what we want to do! I promise you and I promise myself: we will—from tonight—we will live again, and we will love again, and perhaps the most precious thing, we will laugh again.[1]

And that is a power greater than ourselves! It lifts up our valleys and levels the uneven ground of our lives, making the rough places a plain. There is no other, none besides God, who calls our name.

"Grace to you, and peace, from God," who is our true Father and Mother.

Suggestions for Prayer or Journaling:

1. Where in your life has woundedness brought you to the place of truly realizing God's gracious love for you?

2. Journal about an experience you found to be very humbling in your life. Would you change any of the events? How?

Seeing the Light

Read and reflect: Acts 9:1–20; John 21:1–19

I can't think of any biblical text that more clearly fits the second step than this description of Paul's conversion experience. First of all, it teaches us that coming to believe in a power greater than ourselves is just that: a *process* that happens as we are on a journey. As one book puts it, "faith is a verb."

One of the things we notice as we look at the text is that, like Paul, we experience being pulled toward evil on our journey. Paul thought he was a man of faith. He tried to "get it right" by keeping all the Judaic laws, and he was persecuting Christians because they were teaching that "getting it right" was no longer the point—that faith in Christ, simply trusting that we are loved even without "getting it right," is the point.

When Paul sees the light from heaven and is knocked to the ground by its power, Jesus identifies himself only very briefly as the one whom Paul has been persecuting, so that he can make the connection there between his persecution of the followers and of Jesus himself. The greatest persecution of Christ and of Christians is by those who think they know God but don't. But then without any long theological discourse—and I think that's important to note—Jesus simply says, "Rise and enter the city and you will be told what you are to do." That is, "Keep on truckin'!" We just keep on keeping on after such a revelatory experience, and God's will and plan for us will be unfolded. It may not unfold as we had intended, but it will be God's leading us by the hand as we simply put one foot in front of the other. As someone said in my office recently, as the session took a totally different direction than she had anticipated, "This isn't anything like I had planned!" It seldom is!

One thing we notice in the seventh verse is that we are told that the people who were traveling with Saul (Paul's earlier name) heard the voice, but saw no one. That says to us that those around us, even very close to us, will not experience God the same way we do. We each have our own conversion experience. God speaks to each of us in the way we can best hear; others may not experience the same thing in the same way. That is one of the principal teachings of St. John of the Cross as well.

Next, we have Ananias, a disciple already at Damascus, but who knows nothing about all this, being spoken to in a vision by Jesus and told to go to the street called Straight and find Saul and lay hands on him so that he might regain his sight, which he lost in the experience of light on the road. Ananias knows Saul to be chief persecutor of the new Christians and says, in effect, "Are you kidding?" But Jesus says, "I know what I am doing, and you will be surprised whom I'll use to do my work." So Ananias listens and obeys without debating it anymore. That's what spiritual writers call "humility."

Ananias does as he is instructed, and immediately the scales fall from Saul's eyes, and he regains his sight. One thing we see in this passage, then, is that in the Christian community, when others listen and obey in humility, there is great power that works through them to heal us. When another cares for us and touches us, the scales fall from our eyes, and at last we too can see.

That having the scales removed from our eyes is not exactly fun though, we would all agree from this narration of events, if not from our own journeys! It seems from this text that God is not so concerned with our *comfort* as with our *conversion*. Even though Paul thought he was doing God's will before, and that he was a man of true faith, he was mistaken. His zealousness was actually evil.

The subject of evil comes up again and again, and we struggle to come to understand it in ways that are not reductionistic cartoon caricatures of a red-horned and red-tailed devil figure. One way I've come to see evil is as a moving away from the light toward darkness. Evil is always very subtle and hard to discern, especially in ourselves. In our Bible study group at church, we had a kind of built-in visual aid because the library where we meet has a dimmer switch that is very sensitive. I got up and started gradually dimming the lights and asked people to tell me when they first noticed the difference in the amount of light. I turned the switch about 180 degrees before anyone could perceive, from the room environment itself, that a change was taking place. Moving toward darkness is like that. It can take place very slowly and gradually and not even be noticeable to us for a while. One day we look up and find ourselves in darkness.

What we know about the journey is that God has ways of moving us out of that darkness into a light that is so intense we are at first blinded by it. And this happens just as we are breathing our threats against others! Conversion is God's doing and comes upon us like a bolt out of the blue. It may come in quieter ways than Paul's experience, but even in the quiet, conversion is a bolt out of the blue!

Maybe Jesus just lays out a new way to be about our work and life that works better for us. Like the fishermen in the gospel text from John, if we listen to Jesus' direction for our life, the result may surprise us. In that text Jesus comes to the fishermen as they are out in their boats and is somehow able to see below the surface to what is really there. Now these men fish for a living; this is what they do. And Jesus was a carpenter. Do fishermen not know where the fish are? Do fishermen listen to a carpenter? This carpenter is somehow able to see below the surface to what is really there, and if we listen to Jesus' direction for our lives, we may hear him laying out a new way to be about our work and life that is more productive. For those of us whose primary addiction is workaholism, that is good news!

At a workshop on the healing of memories, conducted by Dennis and Matthew Linn, we wrote out a dialogue with Jesus in which we laid out a burden we were feeling and asked for his help and lifting of it. I wrote about how I can so easily get my own co-dependency hooked in my ministry and begin trying to meet too many diverse expectations, walking on eggshells trying not to step on anyone's feelings, and being really drained by it all.

Jesus wrote back, "Sit in your new hot tub with me and bask in my love. Enjoy the water and warmth and just rest in my arms. I am the living water, bubbling, yes, brimming over with new life. Come to me!"

Now that's not exactly what I expected to hear! But I know God is a God of surprises, so I begin and end each day now in our hot tub for a half an hour or an hour that "bookends" my day. And the paradox is that in the slowing down, I have more time and am more organized than I've ever been. I have been freed up to let go of thinking I have to write personal letters to everyone who inquires about what I'm doing here, and instead I've now written out one "generic" letter which I send to pastors who write requesting the information that used to take me over an hour each to compile and prepare.

The point is, nothing in God's ongoing conversion process will ever make sense to us. I'll never understand how I have more time now than when I was paddling faster. But the fact is I do, and I'm not questioning it!

In our ongoing conversion, we see things in a new way and are led, like Paul, to make changes in our lives that move us on to new places in our journey. Truly, it isn't like anything we had planned! And that's what the second step means when it speaks of coming to believe that a power greater than ourselves can restore us. Praise God!

Suggestions for Prayer or Journaling:

1. Write out a "time line" of some of your most life-changing "Damascus road" experiences.

2. When and in what way has another cared for you and touched you so that scales fell from your eyes?

3. Journal about a time when God seemed less concerned with your comfort than with your conversion.

4. When was an occasion when your own zealousness was mistaken, was actually *un*-faith. Speak now with God about that. Listen to God's response.

STEP 3

We make a decision to turn our will and our lives over to the care of God as we understand God.

Patience, People

Read and reflect: Job 42:1–3; James 5:7–11

There are two important messages in this reflection. One is the message contained in these scripture passages. The other is the important lesson we all have to learn at some point, that God's word still gets communicated even when the writer hasn't integrated it fully into his or her own being!

When I first started therapy, back in the days before psychologists knew anything about ACOA issues, I spent three months with a man who tried to figure out what the problem was, since I didn't fit any standard diagnostic categories, as they call it. One day he said, "You know, I thought your main problem was anger, but I've been wrong; it's really impatience." That little gem of wisdom was pretty expensive, but right on target.

As I drove around running errands the week this text came up in the lectionary cycle, I pondered by what authority I could stand before my congregation and preach about patience. It was only later in the week that it came to me to turn it around then, and share with them the effects of impatience in my life, and, therefore, in all our lives.

For my main sermon illustration that Sunday I brought with me to church just the most current result of my impatience: what was left of a pair of navy blue Levis I bought my son on Monday— the day, ironically, that I began pondering this text. He wanted faded blue jeans, and I figured: Why pay $45 when I can buy dark ones for $16 and let the dry cleaners fade them for $3? So I took them to the cleaners but they said it would take three days and they couldn't guarantee the final color. I decided I could do it myself quicker than that, and even choose the final color.

So I went home and read the Clorox label. It said you use $\frac{1}{4}$ cup in a washer load. Well, I figured, if a little bit of bleach, diluted, gets things clean, a lot will fade them—and probably the more, the quicker, right? So I gave them a bath in a pan of about a gallon of full-strength Clorox. I discovered that the shades of blue aren't so easy to control, though, and decided then to try for white. That seemed to work, and they were fine, really, until I put them through the wash cycle to get the smell out. I went to bed and forgot all about them until I got home the next night and everyone said, with twinkling eyes, "Have you seen E.J.'s pants?"

I thought they meant how well they turned out. They brought them up to me in this bucket! Shreds of white string connected by rivets. I couldn't believe it.

While the bill was only $16 and not $45, still it called me to judgment once again about my impatience, and I couldn't help but see that perhaps the dry cleaner knows something I don't know about fading jeans, and how long that takes.

The parallel to the life of faith then seemed obvious to me, as I went to my office the next day and read over the week's texts. I—we all—want faith on demand, too. If the whole object of the spiritual life is to be faithful people, well, then, let's have it, God! In one day, please, and a nice medium blue, please.

The only "catch" is that that kind of faith—the instant one-day-service kind of faith—will never make it through the first "wash." When it comes up against the giant agitator post of life, it will be shredded beyond recognition, and we'll be left bare-bottomed in the spiritual breeze blowing around us. And I have *been* there, and I *can* speak with authority about that.

So: how do we move from instant faith to true, deep, real faith?

Just the way we are: slowly, haltingly, painstakingly, enduring through trials and tribulations that come our way. According to James, the very purpose of trial is that faith in God's goodness should become stronger and conquer the troubles themselves.

When the scriptures speak of steadfastness, the notion is always that of those who went through suffering. Faith development is a matter of exercising forbearance and fortitude in the struggles of life, not finding a genie in a magic lamp that will make the struggles disappear.

Job is a classic example—and our primary biblical example—of steadfastness in suffering. You may remember he's the one who had a pretty nice life and was a good and righteous man, then lost it all, and said, "Hey! What is this, anyway? What'd I do to deserve this?" His friends tried to help but their words weren't very helpful

—mainly guilt trips. Finally, God speaks to Job and overwhelms him with a poetic picture of God's incredible power, wisdom and knowledge. God asks things like, "Where were you when I created the world?" "Who decided how large it would be?" "Do you know the laws that guide the stars and direct the Big and Little Dipper?" After about three pages of that, Job says, kind of sheepishly, "Well, gee, I guess I spoke foolishly." Then God goes on for about two more pages, and then Job speaks the passage from this reading: "I have talked about things I did not understand; I knew only what others had told me, but now I have seen you with my own eyes. I'm sorry I didn't trust you."

Seeing God with his eyes does not mean Job had a physical vision of God, but an experience of God that was real and personal and is possible even in suffering, and that conclusion to the book of Job is the real climax of the book. The important end of the book is not that Job gets all his stuff back (which he does) but that he gets his faith back. The point for us as people of God, seeking faith, is that Job was not in the least stoical or unwavering, but he endured. He hung in there. He was steadfast, not meaning that he never wavered or doubted or questioned—because he did—but steadfast in the sense of going through the suffering.

And right there is where all of this faith talk begins to intersect with the recovery process and journey we are engaged in today. There is a connection between the development of faith and the learning to love ourselves. In the painful process of learning to feel our feelings, we begin to know who we are and we have to know who we are before we can love who we are. And, somehow, loving ourselves is inextricably tied to being able to trust God. I thought about it all week, but I just can't explain it. It just is. The closest thing I came to finding something written on it was the September 13 meditation in *Days of Healing, Days of Joy.* It says there:

> If there is emotional or spiritual poverty
> in our lives, the problem is not "out there,"
> it's "in here."

It continues that, as we get in touch with our own specialness, that in turn connects us with the specialness all around us. As we know, personal growth, like the growth of the farmer's seed, takes time.[1]

The "bottom line" for us is that the most important thing we can "do" in the faith journey is to just keep on keeping on—getting in touch with feelings, letting them be there, and knowing that even the seemingly negative things—anger and rage, for instance—are all part of the "irrigation process" that has to take place in order to produce fruit.

When I look back over some of the pain and suffering in my own life, what I can now see, in retrospect, is God's purpose in it. The severe headaches I had at one point eventually put me in touch with the anger I was shoving down, and they forced me to work it through. Being told I would never be able to have children eventually put me in touch with the ways I was repressing the feminine and my sexuality.

At the time of all those scary and crummy experiences, I, like Job, thought God had forsaken me. But also, like Job, I was not there either when the world was formed—or even when bleach and Levis were invented! So we see always, as Paul says, "through a glass darkly." We experience the new being, as the theologian Paul Tillich says, "fragmentarily and ambiguously." In Twelve Step terminology, we do not have the benefit of "understanding" the God to whose care we turn over our will and our lives. God is not a prisoner of our understanding, and to make a decision to turn our will and our lives over to such a God whom we cannot, and *do* not, and *will* not "understand"—this is faith.

Suggestions for Prayer or Journaling:

1. In what areas of your life are you most impatient? What are some of the things that happen as a result of your impatience?

2. Listen to the St. Louis Jesuits' song, "Patience, People." Let it wash over you as you sit and do nothing.

Increasing in Wisdom and Stature

Read and reflect: Luke 2:41–52

The first thing we learn from this gospel lesson is that Jesus was not a perfect little person who knew everything right from the beginning. The text says that Jesus' parents found him in the temple sitting among the teachers, listening to these men and asking them questions. He also had some answers, and all who heard him were amazed at his level of understanding and his answers. But his stance in the temple was one of dialogue: asking and listening, and then understanding and responding. So, asking questions must itself be a form of wisdom, a kind of vulnerability of strength.

At the end of the passage we are told that Jesus increased in wisdom and stature. "Stature" means development, growth, or level of attainment. Wisdom is not the same as knowledge. Knowledge is of and about things, and wisdom is the application of knowledge to life's situations. So what we have here is the scriptures' testimony that Jesus himself was, like us, in process. While he had incredible depth early on, for his age, still he didn't have it all figured out and, like us, had to keep growing in wisdom, had to keep developing, as he got older. For those of us who were taught we ought to imitate Jesus, I find that very freeing. It lends a kind of sanctity to not having all the answers and gives us permission to be, like Jesus, in process, developing as we keep growing older, not already "perfect" as we assumed we were to try to be.

When we say we increase in wisdom and stature, there is an assumption that we're not already fully wise and "finished." Only on the cross did Jesus say "It is finished," and most of us have a lot of growing to do before we're ready to bear that.

The other important thing we learn from this gospel text is that the key to religious learning is in obedience to God alone. Jesus' first and primary allegiance is not to his parents, but to God. He is surprised that they considered him "lost," and asks them, "Where

33

did you think I'd be?" Some commentaries think this story is Luke's way of pointing out to us that "while they were a close family, already a distance had developed between them . . . that already there was a higher call that Jesus was hearing, a voice not theirs that he was attuned to. [This leads then to the] later episodes where Jesus rejects requests from his mother and brothers that he come home. The distance has by then grown too far. He must and will follow the leading not of his earthly family"[2] but of God alone. So already, at twelve years old, the distance between Jesus and the rest of his family is beginning to increase.

For many of us, there comes a voice that calls us along a "road that our parents will not understand, a voice our family will call us away from, and that the neighbors will think is simply wrong."[3] Most of us can affirm that it would be a lot easier just not to hear God's voice. At an open house before Christmas, I was talking with some old friends from the church I grew up in, and they were asking about our church and what I'm doing now. When I explained what we do, I added, "I'm surprised anyone can hear it," because it's hard stuff we do here. This "business" of God that Jesus said he must be about is difficult. It was Dietrich Bonhoeffer, the German theologian who resisted the Naxis, who wrote that the grace Jesus brings us is free, but not cheap. It leads us into arguments with family, friends, colleagues, and neighbors, and eventually to the cross, where "it is finished." And yet Jesus' first priority was to be about God's business.

All of us, especially as people in recovery and working out authority issues, come to the place somewhere along the way where we have to decide anew who really is our authority, and what is our first priority. Jesus found his authority in God, and that gave his whole life a different perspective. If our authority is to be in God's house doing the will of God—to really turn our will and our lives over to God—then loneliness and being misunderstood by friends and family may well be a price that we pay, because the distance increases as others go on their way and we are left behind in the temple.

The good news, though, is that being "lost" is not really being lost. This week a pastor from another denomination was in my office wondering if he could do at his church the sort of thing we're doing here. We got to talking about our own spiritual journeys at one point as he noticed my Zen cushion and asked if I'm doing sitting meditation now. I said, "No, right now I'm in some kind of transition and I'm not sure where I am. I'm on my way *from* something *to* something, but I don't know where that *is* or what it's called. I guess I'm 'lost'!" And we both laughed because we both understood what I meant by "lost."

That is, I'm not lost now in the old scary and unsettling way I used to be lost. I'm lost in some new way that's really OK. I'm in the temple and it's safe here, wherever I am. As I said to him that day, "It feels like I may not know what this is called, but God does, so I'm really not lost." It was so good to be able to say that to someone who understood what I meant.

In this scripture lesson, Jesus was not "lost." His parents did not know where he was, but he was not lost. It was precisely in his being "lost" that his relationship with God was strengthened, and that's the good news: that others' not knowing where we are not only does not mean we're lost, but is probably necessary and important to our growth in wisdom and stature.

If we truly turn our will and our lives over to God, we find ourselves in what one author calls a "cloud of unknowing." It's never clear-cut, I think, exactly where we are, and that's why we try to learn how to discern God's Spirit in our lives. It's not always easy to see where God is, amidst all the furor that is generated by taking an unpopular stand. During the war between the states, someone asked Abraham Lincoln, "Is God on our side?" Lincoln replied, "I'm not concerned whether God is on our side. I'm concerned that we shall be on God's side."[4]

On the first day of each new year, it is customary in the United Methodist Church to renew our covenant with God. We verbalize our decision to turn our will and our lives over to God as we understand God. Only to the extent that we understand God to be someone who cares for us very deeply will we be able to make such a decision and keep it.

John Wesley's covenant renewal service, first held in 1755, was usually celebrated on New Year's Day or on a Sunday near the beginning of the year, and the service always concluded with communion. It parallels very closely the wording of the third step prayer in the AA *Big Book*.

Wesley, in explaining the covenant God has made with us, says that we are sure God's promises still stand because we have known God's goodness and proved God's grace in our lives day by day. On the other side of the covenant, we stand pledged to live only for God, who loved us and gave Godself for us. We meet as generations of Christians have met, "that we may joyfully and solemnly renew the covenant which bound them and binds us to God. Let us, then, remembering the mercies of God and the hope of God's calling . . . give ourselves anew to God."[5]

Inasmuch as peace on earth begins with individual, personal renewal, it is in taking this third step that we truly increase in wisdom and stature.

A COVENANT PRAYER IN THE WESLEYAN TRADITION[6]

I am no longer my own, but Thine.
Put me to what Thou wilt, rank me with whom Thou wilt;
put me to doing, put me to suffering;
let me be employed for Thee or laid aside for Thee,
exalted for Thee or brought low for Thee;
let me be full, let me be empty;
let me have all things, let me have nothing;
I freely and heartily yield all things
to Thy pleasure and disposal.
And now, O glorious and blessed God,
Father, Son, and Holy Spirit,
Thou art mine, and I am Thine. So be it.
And may the covenant which I have made on earth
be ratified in heaven. Amen.

THIRD STEP PRAYER[7]

God, I offer myself to Thee—to build with me and to do with me as Thou wilt. Relieve me of the bondage of self, that I may better do Thy will. Take away my difficulties, that victory over them may bear witness to those I would help of Thy power, Thy Love, and Thy Way of life. May I do Thy Will always!

Suggestions for Prayer or Journaling:

1. In what sense do you feel that you are still holding on, unable to abandon yourself to God?

2. Journal about the similarities and differences between the Wesley prayer and the AA prayer as they might aid your conscious contact with God at *this* time, and in the future as you grow in wisdom and stature.

STEP 4

**We make a searching and fearless moral
inventory of ourselves.**

On Detachment

Read and reflect: Luke 10:1–12, 17–20

Among the offerings at the First National Conference on Co-Dependency in Arizona was a play called "Family Baggage." The promotional material for it pictured two actors struggling under the weight of the several suitcases they were trying to carry. The play is about the "baggage" we all carry as adults from dysfunctional families, and how we need to begin to put some of it down, especially that which no longer serves us on our journey.

I came across that flyer shortly after I'd had a dream one night of a giant bundle—like the kind that cartoon characters carry on a stick, only bigger—and the message was that the excess bulk had to go. In the dream the bundle was getting smaller, and the "baggage" diminishing, with more space now under the cover.

So I was interested to see that the following week, the suggested preaching text in the common lectionary we use was the story in Luke where Jesus urges us to let it all go. When I arrived at a retreat in Minnesota the next week, the first thing the retreat director there said to us was, "It's not what you take away from this retreat that's important; it's what you leave behind."

Truly, leaving behind our excess baggage is the "spiritual awakening" that precedes carrying the message out to others, because whatever we're still carrying within us, we'll carry out to others. Dropping the baggage, though, is not something we do all at once, but in stages and steps. As the retreat director shared with us, at one point in her own life, she was going through a particularly harrowing experience and asked her teacher, "How long is this going to go on?" He replied, "What difference does it make? Then it will just be on to something else."

But each thing we let "up" from our unconscious—each piece of "baggage" we drop—is that much less we carry around.

Detachment is probably the single most important "ingredient" of the spiritual life, because it produces humility, and humility is what brings us to forgiveness and compassion. We discover that everything goes together.

The problem, as I see it, is that while we can read books and see plays about the necessity of detachment, it is something we only really attain by practice. Nobody can carry anyone else on his or her shoulders to the final goal. At most, one can say with the Zen master Thich Nhat Hanh, "Well, this is the path, and this is how I have walked it. You also walk it." Each person has to take every step on the path himself or herself.

I'd like to share here some of what I've learned—the "how-to" —and, maybe more importantly, the how not to, that I've learned from my own detours.

Detachment is letting go of all that we are inordinately "attached" to in life, and it almost follows in a kind of "order." First we are shown our "external" attachments—maybe what we would call "addictions": to food, drink, drugs, spending, jogging, sports, TV . . . whatever we will put up quite a fuss about if it threatens to be taken away from us.

I thought I'd dealt with this level some while back. I've let go of junk food, caffeine, salt, and—most of the time—sugar and chocolate. But if we think we have no attachments to food, God has a marvelous design to test that out: a seven day vegetarian menu! By Tuesday of this retreat called "Silence and Awareness," I was already counting the days until my plane would fly me out of there. One day I glanced up the cafeteria line and saw what looked like cheeseburgers and, at the end of the line, a large bowl of yellow things—could it be potato chips? Like a mirage, it faded as I drew closer to the sign (they always wrote out a hand-lettered sign on a card and put it next to anything that was too weird) and on the card it said, "meatless surprise burgers." I don't really like surprises, but that's all there was to eat, so I tried to pretend this was a cheeseburger . . . until a lentil bean dropped out of it onto my plate. The bowl at the end was full of sliced yellow grapefruit.

One day I went through and saw what looked to me like cottage cheese. I was so excited—until I saw a sign next to it: "Vegetarian." I decided to pass on it, but then spent all of dinner trying to figure out, "What is vegetarian cottage cheese?" Is that from a cow that only ate grass? The energy I had that week around meals revealed my lingering attachments to food.

The next "layer" is internal attachments—attachments to our ways of doing things, to our anger, to old hurts, to old memories . . . and here is where the snag can come in for ACOA's, I think. When I first read John of the Cross, without any direction in interpreting his work, I came to the part about detaching from feelings, and I made a grave mistake that detoured me for the next three or four years. I proceeded to further "stuff" my feelings, calling that "detachment" —and then wondered why I didn't experience the "peace that passes all understanding." Stuffing is not detachment, and I spent the better part of this week-long prayer retreat getting those two absolutely clear in my mind now. To detach from feelings means to let them come up, to feel them and let them be there, but not to wallow in them, not to let the "tail wag the dog," not to drown in them. We have to watch our "all or nothing" tendencies—having decided to no longer "stuff" feelings, now to be attentive to not wallowing in them—to feel them, "note" them, and come back to center.

The third "layer"—a very painful layer to move through—is a spiritual layer, where we detach from the "teddy bear" God who finds us parking spaces and makes sure Baskin Robbins isn't out of rainbow sherbet when we arrive. This is a really difficult "purging" to go through, especially for ACOAs, since it took most of us our whole lives to find enough faith to believe that God was even in the rainbow sherbet. And now we're nudged to let go of having to have nice sweet consolations all the time, and to just look for God, in the pain, in the surfacing of memories, in the confusion and even in the doubt. This is a hard teaching; who can listen to it?

The only way I can "hear" it is to consider the fruits at the end of the process—or nearer the end; there really is no "end" as long as we're alive. If you want to see what this process of detachments works in the soul, I recommend reading some stories about the lives of Zen masters who've gone pretty far with it. One such book is *One Minute Wisdom* by Anthony de Mello, a collection of daily devotional readings about the relationship between a master and his disciple. It doesn't say whether the master is Jesus, or a Zen teacher, or a rabbi, or who; it's left to our imagination. The theme is how silence and awareness, the practice of detachment, truly generate holiness. In the practice of detachment, we discover that everything in life—our angers, our hurts, our loves, our griefs, our obsessions —passes, that everything is constantly changing, that there is nothing we can cling to anyway, except God.

One classic story, not found in de Mello's book, tells of a Buddhist monk's response to the invasion of his temple by marauders. Everyone else in the city is frightened and has fled, but this one monk is not threatened and does not run with the rest. Angered by that, one of the invaders storms into the temple and screams, "Do you know that I could run you through with my sword without losing an eyelash?" To which the monk replies, "Do you know I could *let* you run me through with your sword without losing an eyelash?"

That's what you call "detached." That kind of detachment— from things and family and friends and life itself—is what strengthens us to be in true mission to others. That is what Jesus practiced, in his life and on the cross. His only allegiance was to God.

This kind of detachment is made possible by quieting ourselves down and centering on "the one thing needful." "Our greatest need," writes John of the Cross, "is to be silent before this great God, with the appetite and the tongue, for the only language God hears is the language of love, and love is born out of silence."

We don't need fame, wealth, position, status, or title to come before God. God accepts and loves us just as we are, detached from everything we thought was important or necessary—just as we are, poor, wretched, blind. All we need to find—sight, riches, healing of the mind—we find in God alone. Just as we are, God will receive us, welcome us, pardon us, cleanse us, relieve us. Thanks be to God.

Suggestions for Prayer or Journaling:

1. Close your eyes and focus on your breathing. Sit with your feet flat on the floor, your knees lower than your hips, back straight, chin tucked slightly in. As thoughts, sensations, sounds, or feelings vie for your attention, simply note "hearing," "resentment," "impatience," "itching," "remembering," "thinking," or whatever the interruption is, and return to your experience of simply breathing, neither hanging on to that which seems "good" nor pushing away that which causes concern. Without

judgment, remain focused simply on your breathing. Expand your time spent in this way until you practice it 20 to 30 minutes each day. Morning is a preferred time, but whenever you can create the time is helpful.

2. Journal about your primary external, internal, and spiritual attachments; then write a dialogue with Jesus about them.

Deliver Us from Evil

Read and reflect: Matthew 4:1–11

One of the disturbing things about the biblical account of Jesus' temptation in the wilderness is that the story says, "Jesus was led up by the spirit into the wilderness to be tempted by the devil." In Mark's account of this incident, the verb is even more direct: Mark says the spirit "*drove* Jesus into the wilderness." In the Greek translation of that text, the meaning is to be *thrown* into the wilderness.

I understand this to mean that God not only allows us to be tempted, but places us in situations where we will face temptation, almost as a prerequisite test of faith before we are to be strong enough to move on to somewhere next in our lives. For sure, that is the way it all took place in Jesus' own history and chronology. This temptation in the wilderness precedes all the work and teaching Jesus later does in the power of God.

But what kind of God "throws" us into the wilderness to experience the full force and power of evil? Perhaps an analogy to human parenting can be helpful in grasping that truth. Our son and daughter will soon be off to college. There they will be tempted on many planes: academically, socially, and sexually. They will be tempted to "get" good grades in ways that are not of God. They will be tempted to move into the bar scene. They will be tempted to use their sexuality in ways that are not congruent with spirituality.

Do we love them? Yes. Do we *allow* this temptation? We will not only allow it, we will drive them down there personally, and pay big bucks to keep them there, in the certainty that this temptation in the wilderness precedes all the work and teaching they will later do in the power of God.

So the question is not whether we will be confronted with evil, but how to recognize it when it happens and how to deal with it. Two things are clear from this gospel account. First, evil comes in the form of what looks very tempting to us. This story uses the noun "tempter" to describe the evil that is often personified as "the devil" elsewhere. And, second, this tempter is extremely subtle—as the Genesis story reminds us, "more subtle than any other wild creature that God had made."

So we can expect evil to look very tempting to us, and we can be aware that it will present itself to us as perhaps an angel of light. That is, it may surprise us that it has shades or elements of truth along with it so that it is just convincing or confusing enough to win us over if we're not awake and ready. It will present itself to us in ways or through people we least expect. So we must need some protection against its power and cunning.

I have noticed an interesting change of direction and surprising refocus in recent ACOA recovery tapes I've been listening to by some of the major writers and workshop presenters in the field. These specialists in the co-dependency recovery process, who have always taken plenty of jabs at the institutional church, are beginning to steer ACOAs and other co-dependents in recovery back to their church or synagogue.

While I can only speculate on their reasons for this change of direction, I think at least part of the reasoning is the realization that, with no theological or spiritual direction, and no scriptural or historical grounding, ACOAs are left out in the wilderness blowing around in the spiritual winds with no real roots and are prey to the tempter's subtleties that can become then the incarnation of evil in their lives in powerful and destructive ways.

It's important to notice that in this gospel story, Jesus responds to the tempter not out of some personal opinion, but out of his grasp and internalization of scripture. Three times he counters the tempter's challenges with the words, "It is written . . ." and then follows with words handed down from the tradition.

The tempter then, catching on to that right away, begins to quote scripture also. Again, Jesus' grasp and internalization of the scriptures, as opposed to the tempter's literalistic surface understanding, is what counters the temptation.

I've been pondering the nature of the temptations that come to co-dependents for some time now, since Terry Kellogg, in a tape I was listening to on hidden anger in recovery, made a statement that connected with some of my own current thoughts. He made this important observation there:

In co-dependency, we're blowing it. We're teaching people that what they do—that is, caring and giving and being
helpful to others—that that's co-dependence, and I really
do believe that co-dependents can carry that too far. The
co-dependents' problem isn't how much they give and
care for others; the problem is that they can't give to and
care for *themselves.* . . . If we cured all the co-dependents
the way we want to cure them nobody would be doing
anything for or giving a *squat* about *anybody.* What is
going to be important in recovery from co-dependency is
not that we stop giving and caring for others, but that we
learn to give and care for ourselves. True spirituality is
self-forgiveness. Co-dependents try to forget themselves
before they ever remember themselves. In recovery from
co-dependence, we develop a sense of self-identity and
awareness—"know thyself"—and once you know yourself, you can forget yourself and have true spirituality.
You can then give to others. Only when we give before we
can give, then that's co-dependency.[1]

Notice the way Kellogg understands spirituality in the biblical
sense that Jesus taught and lived: self-giving love as the ultimate
goal of life. There is no sense in his talks on co-dependency that "I
do what I need to do for me, and when I don't 'get,' I abandon."

While it's true that the recovery process helps us to firm up the
self, the temptation we face as co-dependents is to worship and serve
only the God of our recovery, and to forget what it is we are moving
toward as Christians throughout our lives. Once recovery becomes
that to which we give our allegiance, then our true identity as sons
and daughters of God, as believing people, is under attack. We are
tempted, as Jesus was, to deny who we are and what we believe to be
God's will and purpose for our lives.

We will be tempted, for example, to make amends not because
we feel contrition for the harm we've caused another, but because
making amends to them is good for *us.* Think back, for a moment,
to the last time you were on the receiving end of that kind of
"amend" and be in touch with why you resented and resisted receiving it. It smacks of being *used,* not *loved.* The actions may look
the same, but the underlying motives are very different.

As I pondered other temptations that come to us, it seemed

that different temptations present themselves to us at different times in our journeys. For instance, in the early stages of our recovery, we will be tempted to look for rules to follow in the spiritual life and transfer our need to "get it right" into the spiritual realm, creating a works righteousness that is precisely what Jesus came against.

Later on, especially if we don't pay attention to our tendency to extremes of "all-or-nothing" kinds of thinking, we will tend to flip-flop over to deciding there is no external authority and that now *we* are the "rule." There is a kind of grandiosity in this; it serves neither us nor others very well. It is true that in the final stage of faith, according to James Fowler's schema, the individual's will is God's will and the two become one, but it is also true that most of us have a long way to go before we are "stage six" people.

How will we know when we're there? We'll be ready and willing to hang on the cross or be assassinated to further God's purposes. Until that time, we can safely assume that we are not the will of God and that, like other mortals, we need to discern that will daily in our lives through our decisions and choices.

We are helped to discern God's direction in our life through spiritual direction, and every spiritual director I've ever had has also been in spiritual direction himself or herself. The older the directors, in my experience, the closer to God they are, and yet the less they presume to know or to be God. Those who, in my experience, are closest to being the will of God are the least sure themselves that that is so.

There are other temptations we face, as co-dependents and Twelve Step participants. Terry Kellogg says one tendency we have is to get "stuck" in our feelings and remain in catharsis, mired down in "catharting." Another temptation is to project "mother" or "father" onto everyone out there who is in a nurturing or authority position, and then nail them to the cross every time they fail to be our mother or father. Kellogg especially warns us not to look for gurus. Find, instead, mentors, he suggests, who can provide what we missed, but choose several—lots of them—so as not to crucify any one person who can never meet those expectations. We need to accept what this person can give us and that person can give us, but not ask or expect what people cannot give. No one person can provide the nurturing we long for.

I know when I was in seminary, I was so disappointed that no one professor provided everything I was trying to understand. I ended up, as God would have it, with one who taught me Jung and theology, one who was my mentor in the spiritual and mystical disciplines, one whose strong suit was in liturgy and one who helped me find grace in the scriptures; and now my parishioners in this setting, teach me about real life in the church. The grace in not having it all "my" way was that I now have relationships with many people instead of just one, and all have provided "pieces" of the mentoring I need.

Another temptation we meet is the temptation to isolate ourselves and call it "solitude," or to continue in a victim role because it's easier than changing, and then justify that to ourselves as "bearing our cross." Jesus, however, was not a victim, and the cross for him was freely chosen.

Another temptation we all face is the temptation to cling to a negative self-image, continuing to devalue ourselves because we can thereby avoid facing the reality of our potential as empowered people.

We can be tempted in the Twelve Step program to think that not communicating our silent judgment of others is "accepting them where they are," when honesty in relationship would be something else that would require facing and dealing with conflict and confrontation. It's important to notice the way Jesus deals with the tempter in this passage. He does not ignore or avoid the confrontation. He faces and deals with it squarely.

It is tempting for us, when we can't understand something, to assume the problem is "out there" and not "in here." That is why, in the fourth step, we talk about a "searching and fearless" inventory. It's important that we not have to fear what we might find when we look, clear-eyed, within.

As co-dependents, we are often tempted to put our interpretations on other people's behavior. I know that in our family that is the single most troublesome thing we "do unto others," and we all hate having it done unto us.

Finally I think we are tempted as co-dependents to avoid self-responsibility. We are somehow always waiting for others to take care of us and resenting the fact that they don't. In my first year of ministry, I used to get so frustrated if I walked into the sanctuary at 8 A.M. on Sunday morning and saw the space set up with little rigid square rows, when we're all trying to get out of our little rigid square ways. But it was many moons before I took the responsibility for drawing the janitor a diagram of what I did want, and speaking to him about it.

Now when I come in and see things set in a way that I think is aesthetically distracting, I do what needs to be done to change the setup. If time is short or I forget, and notice in the middle of the service that something didn't get done, it feels OK to just own that, because it is really God who is ultimately in charge here.

What we can be sure of is that the wilderness experience of being tempted in the spiritual life is not just a literal forty day ordeal which we pass through, not to be returned to it. Forty days, throughout scripture, is a time period used simply to mean a long time, and for us, as for Jesus, we are delivered from evil when we say with Jesus: "It is written, you shall worship the Lord your God, and God only shall you serve."

Suggestions for Prayer or Journaling:

1. Reflect on a time in your life when you allowed someone you loved very much to be in his or her own wilderness. What was the outcome? Can you see God doing this in your life? What is the feeling?

2. What subtle temptations are presenting themselves to you at this time in your life? How do you think Jesus would respond to them?

3. Close your eyes and visualize yourself standing with Jesus in the desert. The tempter has left and Jesus is speaking to you, giving you counsel about how to conduct yourself in the spiritual life. Listen to his teaching. Journal what he speaks to you.

STEP 5

We admit to God, to ourselves, and to another human being the exact nature of our wrongs.

I Have Called You Friends

Read and reflect: 1 John 5:1-6; John 15:9-17

In the movie "Permanent Record," a teenage boy, David, commits suicide. David, a gifted musician, is surrounded by people from his social group at high school, and there are parties and plays and all kinds of gatherings. But, from the beginning of the movie, something is obviously bothering him, and it was never clear to me what that was. David is unable to express to his friends the dis-ease in his spirit, and eventually he commits suicide. The remainder of the movie deals with the aftermath of this act—the premature death of a gifted sensitive musician—on the people he leaves behind. At one point, his best friend finds a suicide note which says, simply:

> Chris—I wanted everything to be perfect.
> It wasn't.
>
> David

And in those words we have some essential clues to the problem, both in our society and in ourselves, of despair, because nothing is perfect and nothing is going to be. We are finite, fallible creatures in this world, and to want perfection is to want to be God; and that is the ultimate idolatry.

So the goal can never be to achieve perfection, but must rather be to live in the world committed to love in the midst of our imperfections. That is all that God asks of us. And, as John says, the commandments of God are not burdensome once we realize that we are able to follow them *because* we are loved rather than *in order to be* loved.

For whatever is born of God overcomes the world; and this is the victory that overcomes the world, our faith (1 Jn 5:4).

That means that what is important is not that we be perfect, but that we trust God's love in our imperfection. That's all.

It means—and this is why honesty becomes the crux of the life of prayer—that all we have to do is be honest before God, ourselves, and others about what it is that is in and on our hearts—simply to be who we are: finite, fallible, creatures before the creator, and to be able to admit that.

In the movie, David's principal tells the school superintendent. "His friends didn't even know him. Why didn't he tell them what was wrong?" The superintendent replies, "Maybe he couldn't. Maybe that's the problem." That is precisely the problem for all of us. It is not our problems that bring us to despair. All you have to do is watch Joni Erickson, the gifted artist paralyzed in a diving accident, paint pictures holding a brush between her teeth to realize that we can live with anything. The problem occurs if we can't share it, if we can't talk about it with others. The fact is, it is harder and more painful not to share who we are, to keep it all in. Keeping secrets is what kills people. And it kills the life of the spirit within us.

Carl Jung says it acts as a psychic poison. He says that "all personal secrets have the effect of sin or guilt, whether or not they are, from the standpoint of popular morality, wrongful secrets. [And in the same category] another form of concealment is the act of holding something back. What we usually hold back are emotions or affects."[1] Whatever it is that we hold back blocks us spiritually and keeps us from deepening in the life of prayer.

To whom, then, do we confess our secrets? Jesus says, "No longer do I call you servants, but I have called you friends, for all that I have heard from God I have made known to you." Many ACOAs do not understand what it means to have Jesus as "friend" —my parishioners have told me that—so in order to get a sense of what that means, let's consider what qualities our friends immediately around us and in the Twelve Step program bring to us. What does it mean to be called "friend"? Whatever we determine that means with our physical friends here, God then must be at least that.

If someone asked me to define a friend, I'd do it this way: When you simply be who you are, in all your not-yet-ness, and then you look around you after a while of that and see who's still around, your friends are whoever is still there. A friend just loves us because we are, not because of what we do. I shared with a retreat group once that, before my recovery began, I used to get lots of notes and cards telling me how wonderful I was, and that now that's mostly stopped, and that it feels pretty healthy—because my motives in doing for others were all confused. Now when I'm doing what I need to do for me, my friends are those people who haven't left.

In the last meeting of the Pastor-Parish Relations Committee here at the church, I was lamenting that I do not seem to have the time for in-home visitation that I had anticipated or expected to be doing. The committee's response was that increasing my hours into a pastoral workaholism is not a mode that my congregation would like to have me set as a model here. We never did resolve the problem of visitation, which is certainly an important part of pastoral ministry. But the message I received is that the resolution is not going to come in a way that blocks my own spirituality and growth in recovery. One of the members, who stopped by the office one Sunday and found me still there at 3:30 in the afternoon, sat down and said, "When do you take time for yourself?" That was the week I began to pay attention to my days off and begin taking them.

These are friends, and Jesus is like that. It's only out of this kind of understanding of God's love that we can understand the Bible verses about following God's commandments. We don't follow them in order to be loved; we are able to follow them because we are loved in this way. It makes all the difference in the world. And the irony of it all is that, as we do what we need to do for ourselves, we will be what others need, too. I went to see the movie "Permanent Record" for myself, but out of that came this word that addresses us all with the question, "What is a friend?"

When I went to Florida recently, I spent the first night with a friend in Cincinnati. Having spent the day in spiritual direction going over some dreams, I was exhausted when I arrived, and she had planned for us to go contra dancing that night. What I really wanted to do was take a shower, wash my hair, and read a book my spiritual director had recommended. My first co-dependent thought was to try to fit myself into the plans she had for us. Fortunately, I felt secure enough in this twenty-year friendship to say honestly how I felt; and so she went contra dancing and I took a shower, read a book and was in bed by nine. It felt so good to be who I am in that friendship. That's the way it is in relationship with God.

We can say what we need and trust that our needs will be met. God does not want a co-dependent relationship with us where we dance around trying to please God. God wants intimacy with us.

We don't know too much about intimacy in relationship, not only as co-dependents, but as a society in general. In a healthy relationship, we can trust that the other will be there for us even in apparent absence. It takes time to develop this kind of trust in a friendship, whether with God or with people. When I left my friends on Sanibel Island where I spent one weekend of my recent trip to Florida, I drove off for the first time in years without sadness. Most years—and I go down every March or April to visit them—I have pulled out of the driveway with a sense of sadness that now we're leaving each other. This year I was surprised to find that, finally, I trust the relationship to hold together even across the miles and months until I see them again. It was as if I was going to the store for bread and milk and will be back. And I will. A week or so later, I received in the mail a book I had left lying on the sofa which I had borrowed from their church's library. No letter was enclosed and no instructions about returning it—just the book in the mail, as if I were now in the other room.

Last year they were in Columbus shortly after my graduation and ordination, and though I missed their stop at our house, they left me a copy of the New English Bible as a present. It was the only translation I didn't yet have. They couldn't have known that. That was God's gift through them. We are bound to our friends not on the basis of any affinity for them, but on the basis of being bound to God! Our friends are the expression of that love that is God's love. Once we experience God's unconditional love, we can look at what we are and what we do and own it without fear.

One afternoon as I was preparing an audio-visual worship service, the screen collapsed as I was setting it up and it ripped off the roll about four inches at the top. I don't know what I did, but I know I was the only one around messing with it when it happened! Then the projector bulb was burned out, so I went to get that replaced. The next week, when I returned the equipment to the seminary from which I had borrowed it, the temptation was to not own all my wear-and-tear on the equipment; but because I have been so loved there, it was really not burdensome to own the damage. In response I received, instead of a rap on the knuckles, an apology for the inconvenience and a promise of reimbursement for the bulb. No word was ever said about the damage to the screen.

For this is the love of God, that we keep God's commandments, and they are not burdensome.

On my Cursillo Weekend, which is an ecumenical renewal weekend that runs from a Thursday night to a Sunday night, we sang "What a Friend We Have In Jesus." At that time, twelve years ago now, I could not relate much to the language of the song, but by the end of the weekend I was beginning to get a sense of what Christian community means, and now the words mean a great deal to me:

Have we trials and temptations?
Is there trouble anywhere?
We should never be discouraged;
take it to the Lord in prayer.
Can we find a Friend so faithful
who will all our sorrows share?
Jesus knows our every weakness;
take it to the Lord in prayer.

It is still very difficult for me to share my feelings with people. In my recovery, it is often only with God and perhaps one other person that I can share the depths of what I feel. But every time I risk that and open to just one person, I find to my surprise that I was not alone after all.

I received a call recently from one of our journaling workshop participants who gave me permission to share this incident. She was calling to ask if she should not come on Tuesday, since she'd fallen so far behind in her work and had not kept her commitment to do the workbook pages assigned around the Fourth Step. She said, "I don't know anyone who is this far behind!" I said, "How about the person at the other end of the phone from you right now? I am further behind than anyone and I'm leading this thing." When we got to the workshop that night, we checked it out and discovered that almost everyone was behind. Only one person in a group of thirty-three was where we were supposed to be! We laughed together and then did what we needed to do about it—extended the assignment to allow more time. The journaling workshop is a tool for growth; it is not meant to be burdensome. When we check out what is "normal" we find, often, that *we* are!

> *Are* we weak and heavy laden?
> Cumbered with a load of care?
> Precious Savior still our refuge;
> take it to the Lord in prayer.
> *Do* your friends despise, forsake you?
> Take it to the Lord in prayer.

In God's arms, God will take and shield you and you will find a solace there. Prayer is not a burden or a duty; it is a privilege. Carry everything to God in prayer.

Suggestions for Prayer or Journaling:

1. Write an "inner wisdom dialogue" with Jesus. Simply begin by writing your name and speaking what you wish to say or share. Then write "Jesus" on the next line and listen for what comes to you. Write the words that come into your head without debating or analyzing. Continue until you have carried everything to him in prayer.

2. What qualities do you value in a friend?

3. An excellent resource is Paul Hinnebusch's *Friendship In The Lord.* You may wish to read it and write your reflections about its application to your life.

Fear Casts Out Love

Read and reflect: Matthew 21:1–11; 26:14–27:66

Many of us, I suspect, have often seen the cross more as something done to us rather than for us. That kind of perspective prevents us from being in touch with the ways we too shout with the crowd, "Crucify him!" One thing I'm very clear about is that we will not experience the power of Easter morning until we are present at the place called Golgotha and begin to realize our participation in that event.

I used to hate Good Friday services. The liturgy always has some recollection of this passion story in one form or another, and usually we, the congregation, were written in somewhere to shout, with the ancient crowd, "Crucify him!" I could refuse to participate, and often did, either by my silence or by my non-attendance. Like Peter, I thought smugly to myself, "Though they all fall away, I will never fall away; even if I must die with you, I will not deny you."

I have been conscious since at least kindergarten of such a longing for God, and I couldn't imagine rejecting that kind of love, if I could ever find it. And yet, somewhere deep down in the core of my being, I had to remain open to the possibility that there was something more to all this than I could presently grasp. Why would people crucify God's love? It's only been in the past few years now that I've really been in touch with the ways I, too, have made the sepulcher secure by sealing the stone and setting a guard.

When I stumbled onto the writings of St. John of the Cross, I knew I'd found someone who understood and shared my longing for God. I looked, then, until I found a course on John's work, which was offered at the Methodist seminary by a Roman Catholic priest who was on the faculty there. He was very gracious when I called for permission to take the course, and because I was presently at a seminary with whose denomination he did a lot of work, he seemed to understand the kinds of questions and struggles I was having.

The first day I drove up there to class, I was feeling as if I would never fit into any denomination or church, and was getting into my "What's wrong with me?" mode. When I arrived, late, a woman was just asking him, "What do you have to do to be able to really understand this kind of spiritual writing?" The priest smiled and answered, "Well, first of all, you have to become a heretic!" I knew he meant that this kind of thought transcends the boundaries of dogma, and for me that was a breath of fresh air. From that day, the priest and I seemed to really "connect." In him, I experienced very deeply God's love.

One day, he asked if anyone could explain a poem John had written on the Trinity. As we had read the last verse, I had had a sudden flash of its meaning, but when I tried to put words to it, the explanation just disappeared into silence. He looked at me with such understanding, as if he knew exactly what I hadn't been able to articulate, and why. I never felt so understood as when we were in dialogue together.

He and I began a relationship of spiritual direction, and that summer I transferred to the Methodist seminary, largely because my experience with him and the students in his class had shown me that I was not a freak after all. I could share the deepest parts of myself and my journey with him, and he always understood exactly what I was saying. Sometimes in class when no one seemed to understand him, he would look back in my direction to see if I was tracking with him. Something united us.

While he was very deep, he was also very practical and real. One weekend in late summer, we went up together to a monastery in Michigan where he was preaching. We stayed overnight in northern Ohio on the way, as guests at the house of someone who had read his books and wanted to meet him. The host wanted very much to impress him with an upcoming trip to Rome that he was to make, and was telling us that he was studying Latin in preparation for it. I sat there eating my peas, wondering who speaks Latin these days, but not honest enough to ask. My priest friend replied, unabashedly, "I think you'll find that no one speaks Latin there anymore!" I almost choked! I had never experienced such honest "realness" in anyone or in any relationship before. There was total commitment to truth, in love, in this dialogue, rather than game-playing with some limp smile and a phony response of "That's nice."

In classes when I asked, "What would John of the Cross say about such-and-such?" his face would get red and he would say, "If John of the Cross were alive, he'd be teaching this class, not me!" He admitted his limited understanding of John's thought and work. I learned humility and honesty and lots of spiritual theology from him, and took his courses on the Trinity, symbols, and theologies of salvation.

But eventually my fears began to get in the way—fears that when he retired or I graduated, this relationship would change and I would be hurt; fears that, somehow, it wasn't "normal" or appropriate for a married woman to feel this connected to a sixty-two year old celibate Catholic priest. I don't know what was going on. I certainly wasn't in touch at a conscious level with any of the reasons. Like Peter, I was threatened by what would happen to me if I stayed and owned my half of the relationship. It was easier to start putting the love I was feeling to death, erecting a wall in the relationship, as if that could somehow protect or blunt the pain and threat I feared.

And this is what I think we all do; the cross is something done by us. When love comes to us in powerful ways we "cannot accept the subversive force of [it]. Love breaks down the borders and subverts the constituted order, so it must be annihilated. . . . We must become aware that though we thirst for love, we yet reject it because we fear it, and so take refuge in the flat banality of daily life."[2]

It is love's characteristic that it alters our relationship with reality. "The psychic order we have been used to is suddenly upset. . . . The upheaval of love is all it takes; at that moment we are disoriented, we lose our bearings [as love reveals us to ourselves and confronts us with our rigid attitudes which] melt away like snow in the sun."[3]

And so we try to kill love. We take it out to the dump outside the city gates and nail it to the cross. Then we make the sepulcher secure by sealing the stone and setting a guard at the entrance to the tomb. And we think this is the power we have to kill God's love for us.

If I thought this was just my story, I'd sit on it for five more years. But this is not just my story. This is our story, as ACOAs, as Christians and as human beings; and until we see this in ourselves and acknowledge it before God and others, we will never understand the message of Easter that gifts us with life again out of this very death we have participated in. For Easter is God's "yes," and first we must own our "no." We can only experience the risen Jesus by honestly facing the fact that it is we, also, who crucify Jesus. Today, as in those times, fear casts out love. As we ponder that truth about ourselves, we await God's truth in response to it.

SOLITUDES
by Michele Matto and Robert Baker

Why can't I return your language of the eyes
to risk that you'd be touched
to know that I, too, care as much—
or is it fear: to *both* reveal the depth we feel
might open up an unknown world
that asks me to be real?

Maybe it's myself I fool
to feign a stance so measured-cool
to think a wall like this could hide
the flowing feelings trapped inside,
to think my shield could somehow blunt
the hurt that always rushes in
when solitudes are met and shared
and then called on by One above.

So calm, so cool, I'm nobody's fool
your eyes clear and free
are calling out to me—but can't you see
I must control, I've sold my soul
I'm not prepared to let this scared
and wounded child free.

Maybe it's myself I fool
to feign a stance so measured-cool
to think a wall like this could hide
the flowing feelings trapped inside
to think my shield could somehow blunt
the hurt that always rushes in

when solitudes are met and shared
and then called on by One above.

Fear . . .
    Fear . . .
        Fear . . . . casts out love.

Suggestions for Prayer or Journaling:

1. Write about a time when you have experienced God's love in powerful ways and then attempted to kill or sabotage it. What were the feelings then? What are they now as you recall it?

2. Listen to *St. Matthew's Passion* (available from the listening center of your local library).

3. Read Aldo Carotenuto's *Eros and Pathos,* available from Inner City Books, Box 1271, Station Q, Toronto, Canada, M4T 2P4.

STEP 6

We are entirely ready to have God remove all these defects of character.

Transformation: When Is the Hour?

Read and reflect: John 12:20–33

In my office there is a sculpture called "Transformation." It is a clay vase whose outer layer is splitting away, making room for a smooth white center core to emerge from within. It sits in my office because I need a constant reminder that this process of transformation, which feels just like the sculpture looks, really is a stripping away process acknowledged by others out there in the world, such that there are even art objects fashioned about it. I showed it to someone who was doing a fifth step with me, and it produced the same reaction that I have: a reassuring sense that this splitting away of the old rough outside layers really is going to make way for something smooth and pure to grow up from within.

Jesus speaks of this same process in the gospel text about the grain of wheat that falls into the earth and dies in order to bear much fruit. It is different imagery for the same reality: the old is stripped away so the new can emerge.

Now the question is, "Are we ever 'entirely ready' for this stripping away to take place?" It sounds pretty great, doesn't it, to be ready to ask God to take away shortcomings and defects. How many would vote for that? It's like when our kids ask us to take a splinter out of a finger. "Oh, sure, let me get the tweezers." Then there's a moment of panic when they rethink that request as they realize what tweezers will mean. Can't the splinter come out without any more pain? They thought they were "entirely ready" to have it removed, but if removing it may mean that things get stirred up under there a little, then—well, maybe not *entirely* ready!

Actually, I think the splinter analogy is really good for this whole process. Think about it with me some more. To leave the splinter in will mean the wound won't be aggravated by stirring it up with the tweezers; but if the splinter is left in too long, and new skin grows over and covers it, then you have to get a needle and dig it out—and now you're talking blood! Sometimes if a child is too young to understand all the ramifications of just leaving the splinter in, you may have to just hold him or her down with a love that will not let him or her go.

So this process—both the process of having splinters removed and the process of transformation—is never a matter of "if." It is only a matter of "when." The splinters in our personalities that block our receiving and giving of love will have to go if we seek wholeness.

And that's where I think the important word of this gospel text intersects with some important information we now have about how personal transformation proceeds: first, that, paradoxically, we need to have ego strength for the splitting and dying process, and, second, that the process goes on largely at an unconscious level.

What happens in the journey to wholeness is that the ego needs to learn to cooperate with the deeper self that is rooted and grounded in God. Thomas Merton referred to prayer as the movement from the "false self" to the "true self," and that true self is what Jesus was in touch with that enabled him to die like the grain of wheat he describes in the text.

In *The Twelve Steps—A Way Out,* a journaling workbook, the sixth step is described in this way: "We must relinquish our egos and truly seek God's will for us. . . . It is not an action step that we actually take. It is a state of being that takes us."[1] And that is precisely the rub, because the ego does not like to be taken anywhere; *it* does the driving, thank you!

It's not that we need exactly to relinquish our egos, for the ego does have its place in keeping us reality-centered. But it is that the ego needs to cooperate with the authentic self which sees the bigger picture of life, and which is both the center and the circumference of the circle we call the personality. It becomes easier to let that process happen when we understand both the necessity for cooperation and the process of cooperation.

The Twelve Step journaling workbook also says that for some of the more deeply-rooted defects, we may find it necessary to become detached observers.[2] When we observe ourselves thinking negatively or doing something that is not constructive, we can note that and pray for release from that behavior. Using the analogy of the splinter again, we would say that when the splinter is extremely deep, and embedded, and painful enough, even a child can understand that what needs to happen is that the pain must be endured until the splinter is out.

The point is that much of the transformation process is going on at *un*conscious levels, and the readiness to participate in it may be unconscious also. Many people who come into my office are very much feeling the splitting away of the layers—the grain of wheat falling to the ground and dying—but have no idea that the process of transformation is taking place in them. They feel the splitting but are not aware of having been "entirely ready" for this to take place, or even having asked! It is always interesting for me to sit in ACOA meetings and hear people identify which of the Twelve Steps they're "on," as if we really *know* where we *are* in this! There is truly a sense in which all of us are always working all Twelve Steps.

Jesus says, "Now is my soul troubled. And what shall I say? 'God, save me from this hour?' No, for this purpose I have come to this hour" (Jn 12:27). In both Jesus' life and times, and in our own, *we* do not determine the hour. *God* determines the hour. "For everything there is a season and a time for every matter under heaven. . . . A time to be born and a time to die, a time to break down and a time to build up . . ." (Eccl 3:1ff). We know only that a grain of wheat, if it is to bear fruit, is first ripe. So whenever is our hour, the time is right.

When the seed is ready (whether it knows it or not) it goes into the ground and apparently disappears into darkness, apparently breaks down, apparently splits apart. And what emerges out of this breaking down is a whole new being. And God's name is glorified.

Transformation: When is the hour? Who is ever "entirely ready"? Being entirely ready implies trust, faith, and belief that the one we are going to ask will fulfill our request. But being "entirely ready" never provides the answers to how this process will take place in us, and never provides guarantees that it will proceed without any additional pain or suffering for us.

But at that hour and in the process, there is a love, like that which we have for our children with splinters in their fingers, a love that will not let us go, a love that seeks us through the pain. We trace the rainbow through the rain, and feel the promise is not vain, that morning shall be tear-less.

Suggestions for Prayer or Journaling:

1. Do you think Jesus was "entirely ready" for the cross?

2. Read Psalm 22 each day this week as a morning and evening reflection.

3. What do you believe at this time in your life that you *are* "entirely ready" to accept toward your further growth? Journal about it.

We All Are Being Changed

Read and reflect: Luke 9:28-36; 2 Corinthians 3:12-4:2

These readings from the Bible have a common thread: they speak to us of what a transforming experience it is when we encounter God. Each passage tells us something about what we can expect to happen in and after encountering God directly. Both readings pose the question of what it means to be "entirely ready" for the changes God works in our lives—what we call the Sixth Step.

Let us reflect on Luke's account of the transfiguration story and notice, objectively, what takes place. Jesus takes his friends up to a mountaintop, away from the noise and all, to pray. There Jesus prays, but Peter, James and John are too tired and fall asleep. They wake to see Jesus in full glory, his clothes dazzling white in appearance, and talking to two prophets whom they recognize as no longer alive. I mean, this is not your basic Saturday afternoon hike! Peter, who doesn't know what's going on, but feels the need to say something, blurts out something like, "Whoa! All right!" and then a cloud comes and overshadows them. And they are afraid as they enter the cloud. A voice comes out of the cloud—the voice of God —saying, "This is my man. Listen to him!" And then they get real quiet, and they don't say anything to anyone about the whole experience. In an instant, they are changed people.

The first thing I asked myself when I reflected on this text was: When James and Peter and John went up there, were they "entirely ready" for all that? I got out the book, *The Twelve Steps for Adult Children*,[3] to read about the Sixth Step again, and found that it sheds some light on this passage.

The anonymous author of this book says that the Sixth Step is not an action step that we actually take. It is a state of being that takes us. As we live the Twelve Steps daily, we gradually and unconsciously become ready to be changed. What sometimes happens is that we are not aware of being ready to have our defects removed or of asking God to remove them. The first awareness we have is that we are different somehow. We have changed. Often the change is noticed by others before we become aware of it ourselves. Much of this change is accomplished without conscious action on our part.

So, to be "entirely ready" does not necessarily mean to be consciously aware that we are entirely ready, it just means to be entirely ready." It is somehow contingent upon our prior relationship with and trust in God—that is, the first five steps which have preceded it. We can even be dozing off at the time of the action going on, but we will wake to find major transformation going on within and around us.

I think Peter, James and John went up the mountain with Jesus, trusting in their prior relationship with him, and thought they were entirely ready for whatever it would bring them, but I doubt very much if they were "entirely ready" for the way God was going to work a transformation in all of their lives on this trip. In their encounter with God, they are unaware themselves of the change they have experienced, just as Moses was unaware that his face was shining as he came back down from Mount Sinai to the people. Moses' being with God works this change in his countenance. In the Luke account, "Jesus' face is changed as he prays. Jesus' transfiguration, like Moses', unveils the meaning and purpose of his life and ministry."[4] The disciples witnessed this mystery, and their own faith and commitment were deepened.

Think back upon how many times you have set out on what you thought would be an ordinary trip, but later, looking back, you can see now that your life was changed by what happened to you there, and usually not of your own doing. Somewhere and somehow, perhaps in a mysterious way you don't yet understand, you encountered God in that experience and are now changed because of it.

This week I was reminded of the changes that have taken place in my life the past several years as the result of what started out as just an ordinary trip. One night this week I went out to look at used cars, and at one of the dealers I visited, I was surprised to be greeted by an old acquaintance whom I hadn't seen since 1981 when I started seminary. I was surprised to see him there because last time I knew him he was a funeral director, and it seemed like such a change of direction for him to be selling cars. So I asked what he was doing, and he told me he'd burned out. He's a very sensitive man and had gotten very involved with teenage suicides and parents who had lost children, and the emotional toll was just too much. He now just wanted a job where you work from nine to five and leave it there. What I heard in the conversation was that he was starting to take care of himself.

He was equally surprised to hear that I am now a pastor in the institutional church. When he last knew me, I was complaining that I couldn't find God there! He said, "Last I heard you were leaving the Cursillo Community to go to seminary, and that was the 'talk of the town.' " I just laughed and told him I wasn't going to touch that one with a ten-foot pole!

But it got me to thinking, as I drove back across town, truly how much I have been changed in the past eight years. I must have been "entirely ready" to have some of my negative attitudes toward the church and organized religion removed, but I certainly wasn't aware of it. I went to seminary not to become a pastor, but out of my anger that I wasn't learning anything from the clergy. I certainly didn't intend to be one! Even aside from my attitudes, my fears would have stopped me. I would never have believed at that time that an introvert could stand up in front of people every week. When I took the Myers-Briggs Personality Inventory again and came out 29–5 on the introvert/extrovert scale, I concluded the reason our son Aaron was born three weeks early was because I was supposed to have presented a paper in my New Testament class on the day after he was born, and I preferred to go into labor instead.

So, like Peter, James and John, I'm not sure I was "entirely ready" for the transformation that has taken place in my thinking and attitudes and perceptions; I have slept through much of the process, I think, but even that did not thwart the journey.

So, God uses whatever means God deems helpful and necessary to lead us into new perspectives and attitudes. For Peter, James and John, it was a vision; for me it has been dreams and "coincidences." For others it is a myriad of different manifestations of God's very self. In our struggle to understand our experiences, we, like Jesus' disciples, will enter a cloud of doubt and confusion. We, like them, don't always get the message, and need to be reminded to just listen. And, like the disciples, we then return to God and begin the process all over again.

This entire process, or journey, is the life of prayer. Going up to the mountain with Jesus, experiencing the power of God, followed by the cloud of unknowing, is all part of the encounter. We may not know what it's called, and it certainly may not feel like prayer since little of it is spent in the kind of vocal petitionary prayer most of us learned to identify as "prayer," but in all of these things we are being drawn closer to God in prayer. And we are all being changed.

The fact that we are afraid as we enter the cloud, or that we do not understand, does not alter the reality of the process going on. The process transcends our fears and our lack of understanding.

When we ascended into the clouds as we climbed Mount Fuji in Japan, I remember feeling just the way this passage literally describes. It was the strangest sensation to have my feet placed firmly on the ground and yet not be able to see what was ahead and so to feel unsteady. It was very unsettling, and I had to tell myself this was the same kind of cloud I had looked upon objectively from afar the day before when we began the journey, and that being in it didn't alter the fact that we were still safe and okay on firm ground. Moving up into the cloud was part of the journey.

The word "overshadowed" is the same word Luke used back in the beginning of his book to describe how Mary felt when the angel Gabriel spoke to her about Jesus' being born in her. And she, too, was afraid, and not entirely ready to be entirely ready! And yet the birth still took place.

It's the same with our not understanding. A farmer's son one day asked his father, "How do you explain the fact that cows eat grass, grow hair and give milk, and sheep eat the same grass, grow wool, and give no milk?" "I can't explain it," the farmer answered. "It's a mystery. At least it's a mystery to us right now. Maybe someday we'll know; but we don't need to explain it—we just need to use it. So be sure you milk the cows and shear the sheep!"[5]

The transfiguration is a mystery. At least it's a mystery to us right now. Maybe someday we'll know. We don't need to explain it. We just need to use its spiritual gifts. The test of authentic spiritual experience is its fruit. After the transfiguration experience, Jesus "set his face to Jerusalem" and traveled his difficult way to the cross. On our journeys, in the difficult times, we can remember our experiences on the mountaintop, and their memory will help us face the disappointments, frustrations, and persecutions of our daily lives as we follow him. I wondered at the beginning of seminary why God had seemingly showered me with profoundly moving experiences of grace. Was I "special"? Only as time went on did I realize that those experiences were to be the ballast that would preserve my faith when I was alone at sea in later times when authority figures, faculty, friends and family would not—could not—understand what I was about.

One of the times when I would feel the total rejection most clearly was in an encounter with a friend with whom we used to sail on Lake Erie. At the beginning of a three-day sail, when I was captive on his boat, he spoke to me about my interest in the new physics of Heisenberg and Oppenheimer: "Michele, I don't know about some of this *crap* you're getting into."

So, the gospel calls us back into the real world. No, Jesus did not agree to building three booths so they could all stay there and live forever on the mountain top. "We do not live out our lives in the rarefied atmosphere on a mountaintop, but in life's daily events, where the cruciform image gives meaning to our moments of brightest glory and darkest tragedy."[6]

Our lives will be sustained and strengthened by the recalling of our mountaintop experiences. "Our own high and holy moments with Jesus in prayer and worship transform life from a meaningless existence into a purposeful though rugged journey."[7]

And we all, with unveiled face, beholding the glory of God, are being changed into the same likeness from one degree of glory to another. That is, we all are changed when we look upon the glory of God.

Suggestions for Prayer or Journaling:

1. Reflect upon an experience for which you were not consciously "ready" but which God clearly used to transform your attitudes and behavior. What was the outcome? What were your feelings at the time?

2. Read *The Cloud of Unknowing*[8] and keep a journal of the ways in which its thought parallels your own "recovery" experience.

STEP 7

We humbly ask God to remove our shortcomings.

The Foolishness of God

Read and reflect: 1 Corinthians 1:22-25

The journaling workbook *The Twelve Steps—A Way Out* states that "attainment of greater humility is the foundation principle of the ACOA 12-Step Program. It is through humility that we reach the goals as outlined in the steps. The basic ingredient in humility as it applies to the program is a desire to seek and do God's will." But who has known the mind of God? And how can we ever submit to the foolishness of God?

The foolishness of God that Paul is describing in this first letter to the Corinthians is that what appears to us as weakness—a man helpless and powerless, hanging dead on the cross—is actually the strength and power greater than ourselves—the power of God and the wisdom of God—that restores our lives to health and sanity. We preach Christ crucified, a stumbling block and folly to us all!

One day, about my second year of seminary when I was just becoming aware of the fact that the study of the life of prayer was what interested me most and where I wanted to concentrate my energies, there was a notice in the seminary newspaper that there was going to be a panel discussion on "prayer" at which three faculty members and the woman who ran the bookstore would share their own understandings of what prayer is.

The bookstore woman always interested me, because I knew from the books that she ordered and put me onto that she was very deep; I experienced her somehow as a very humble person, and I had been reading enough books by this time to have figured out that humility is the crux of the life of prayer. But none of the books ever explained exactly what humility is. So I went and listened to these four people share their understandings about prayer. Well, three people, actually. Mostly the professors. The bookstore woman mainly listened in rapt attention to the professors' long and scholarly explanations about prayer, and did not interrupt them as they went on and on. I kept hoping someone would define humility, and I waited for one of the four to address it, but no one did. I knew that, whatever it was, the bookstore woman would know. So finally during the question-and-answer time, I asked, "How do you each understand 'humility'?"

The three professors each in turn stated what that word meant to them, but I waited with bated breath for the woman in whom I experienced this quality to tell me what it meant to her. When it came her turn, she just shrugged and said, simply, "I have no idea what it is!" And didn't even try to answer the question.

For some reason, I found that incredibly funny—that the one person in whom I had somehow experienced this "humility" did not know what it was. Her part in the entire discussion was not lengthy or scholarly—nor very enlightening at all, actually—but when I left, I still knew that this was a person of prayer. It all felt like God's little joke to me, and I thought of this passage as I walked to my car: "For God in God's wisdom saw to it that the world would never find God through human brilliance." The foolishness of God!

The place where the Twelve Steps and the scriptures come together is in the understanding that humility is simply the growing awareness that "of myself I am nothing; God does the work." So to "humbly ask God to remove our shortcomings" will mean that we are going to have to come to terms with the foolishness of God about how that removal takes place in us.

One of the paradoxical ways God works is by teaching us to accept our defects rather than to hate them—or to hate ourselves for having them. That is the point Morton Kelsey makes when he talks about our learning to kiss our inner idiot. One piece of God's foolishness is that our dark or shadow side, as Carl Jung calls it, does not go away until we can accept it and embrace it. Trying to shove it away and hating it just makes it loom larger as our own personal bogeyman. Now how could putting your arms around the "yukkiest" part of yourself ever be "redemptive"? Surely we'd just get more dirty, wouldn't we? Only in God's foolishness would such a hug be redemptive.

A woman once shared with me a very important dream she'd had, at a time when she was going through a lot of healing of memories. The dream was, quite appropriately, that she was cleaning house. Three friends were helping her, and when it got to the real dirty work, one, who didn't want to get his hands dirty, was going to leave. She understood that, and said "okay," but told him that she wanted a hug before he left. At first he didn't want to hug her, saying her sweatshirt was all dirty, but she reminded him that "what goes around comes around!" and he then agreed. The other two friends then helped her pack up all the crud they found and put it in garbage bags and set it out for the trash people. What a positive imagery for what's going on in her life! What goes on for all of us in the journey to wholeness! That it is the embracing of precisely that which we want to reject that restores us. Who has known the mind of God?

When we humbly ask God to remove our shortcomings and character defects, then that means, by definition, that we are placing ourselves on God's timetable, and whatever defects and shortcomings remain must somehow belong there, in God's economy. The timing of the removal—or whether it takes place at all—is God's timing. I know that in my own life I have been entirely ready for God to remove my anger and impatience. They bring me nothing but negative repercussions, and no "payoff," and when I began to see, in my reading, a clear picture of what a "holy" person would look like, I wanted to be that, right now. I wanted to be calm and gentle, soft-spoken, mellow, kind and compassionate. I prayed about my character defects—but if you talk to my family, they'll tell you I can act in some very un-spir-i-tu-al ways! Now I don't know what the holdup is here, but I do know now that if God had burned out all my anger at one time, I'd be a pile of ashes right now, because back when I first prayed for that to be removed it made up about ninety-five percent of my personality. So perhaps the delay has been to preserve me by burning the anger off gradually.

I suspect that every character defect that remains in us is being used, while it remains, to God's purposes. I know that when I went to a professor, at one point, lamenting my anger in the environment at the first seminary I attended, he said, "Michele, there is a lot of power in your anger; it can be one of the gifts you bring to ministry, if you can simply learn to channel it." Only years later did I realize that it is precisely my anger that created the ministry to other ACOAs that I now serve. In the foolishness of God, our defects can become gifts! Who knows the mind of God?

One of the first things we learned in seminary was that God would speak God's word despite us. There was a story—a true story —about a seminarian whose two roommates dared him to preach a sermon at his church in which he would name an animal beginning with every letter of the alphabet from A to Z somewhere in the body of the sermon. The seminary student took the bet, and prepared such a sermon, and preached it to his people. In the middle of delivering the sermon, he began to feel really guilty about having turned the occasion of preaching the word into a joke and a bet; but a woman came up to him after the service with tears in her eyes to tell him how much the sermon had spoken to something currently going on in her life. His foolishness became God's foolishness, which is wiser than human wisdom, and has real power to save. In Christ, God has put Godself into our hands, subjected Godself to our abuse—God's apparent weakness. But the weakness of God is stronger than human strength.

I was in a meeting not long ago where a man cried in front of the group, and he apologized, seeing that display of emotion as a shortcoming or defect, somehow. I did not see it that way at all, and I know at least two other men in the group who needed to see a man cry. I thought, as I drove home, that this was where God was in the meeting—in the apparent weakness of this man's tears. For the weakness of God is stronger than human strength. Only in the foolishness of God can the folly of the cross be redemptive.

I once had a dream in which I was flown to a foreign land and was being sold or ransomed off as a slave. I made the sign of the cross as a sign just to myself and God that, wherever this was and whatever was about to happen, I remembered who I am, even though we were all in Middle East dress. A man came up and bought me then, and I wondered what that meant for me at first. But then he looked at me and made the sign of the cross; I made it again too, and knew that I was now safe in his care. I woke up right about there thinking, "How strange a sign of safety—the cross!" I lay in bed trying to recall if the man had signed the cross in the eastern manner, as I do, or western, and I could not remember—I had not noticed. It seemed significant that I could not remember— that it must not be important; for in Christ there is no East or West. Later in the day, I looked up the words to the hymn:

In Christ there is no east or west,
in Christ no south or north;
but one great fellowship of love throughout the whole wide
   earth.
In Christ shall true hearts everywhere their high communion
   find;
His service is the golden cord close binding humankind.
Join hands then, people of the faith, whate'er your race may be.
In Christ now meet both east and west, in Him meet south
   and north;
in Christ all souls are one in Him throughout the whole
   wide earth.

I think that to take the seventh step seriously is to be open to
the foolishness of God—to be open to the depth of the riches of God
and the breadth of the wisdom and knowledge of God, and to accept
whatever follows in God's timetable. "When we humbly ask God to
do the removing, it becomes God's responsibility, and we cannot
accept credit or blame for what follows."[1] For the foolishness of
God is wiser than human wisdom, and the weakness of God is
stronger than human strength, and who has known the mind
of God?

Suggestions for Prayer or Journaling:

1. What character defect would you like to see removed that seems
   to be slow in leaving?

2. Journal about someone you experience as "holy." What is he or
   she like?

3. What is humility for you?

4. Read the poem by St. John of the Cross, "Stanzas Concerning an
   Ecstasy Experienced in High Contemplation."

Twilight Journey Through the Narrow Door

Read and reflect: Luke 13:22–30

"Strive to enter by the narrow door; for many, I tell you, will seek to enter and will not be able."

Through the filter of our unexamined co-dependency, we are likely to hear Jesus saying in this passage, "Shape up and get it together or you'll never get into the kingdom of God." And then, of course, we double our efforts to remove our own character defects so we can be good little saints—and we wonder why our lives are becoming *more* unmanageable.

Jesus' intent in this passage, as I have come to understand it, was quite different from what I had assumed or somehow received by osmosis as I was growing up. In a New Testament class in seminary, we were asked, "What is the 'wide' way? How do *most* of us try to get to God?" And the answer from the class was, "By trying to get it right, by being good and competent in all respects, by getting good grades, etc." "By being trustworthy, loyal, helpful, friendly, courteous . . . brave, clean, and reverent." By following the merit-badge theology that most of us learned as we grew up. And now we realize that as we tried to live that theology out, it generated such pressure that, in our self-righteous anger, we demanded that everyone else remove his or her character defects as well. *That* is the *wide* door!

The narrow door is the way of trusting *God* to remove our character defects, on *God's* timetable, humbly asking *God* to deal with people, places, and situations, and letting go of the presumption that we have to do it all, or that we have to do any of it.

Letting go is an agonizing process for most of us former scouts. (It is interesting to note that the verb Jesus used is "strive," from which we get the word "agonize.") It is not easy to go in through the narrow door of owning our fears, our insecurities, our untrustworthiness, our lack of competence, and to trust that God really loves us and will be with us in spite of ourselves.

As Jesus made his way toward Jerusalem and the climax of his own struggle to be true to God, he was asked whether few or many would be saved. We don't know what the questioner meant by "saved," but from Jesus' answer we can discern what it meant for him. To him, it meant to be able to enter into God's house—to be home.[2]

The "narrow door" to God's house is good news, not bad, because in fact it is the only entry way that is equally available to everyone, regardless of nationality, financial status, respectability, health, or family background.

The narrow door is simply that still, small place in the heart where we say "yes" or "no" to what one knows is true. It is the one place through which no external force can enter to shape or coerce one's choices. It's what Teresa of Avila called the "center of the soul," wherein God dwells.

Because that place is inaccessible to external forces, it is not fundamentally lost or violated even when terrible things happen to us. Traumas may cause us to lose confidence in our center and cause us to look for it in others or in various addictions to which we give our energies. Life may become a long and frantic search for the return of our center, which can only be found, ultimately, *within.*

Finding the narrow door that leads to the center is first and last a matter of being *totally honest before self and God.* In older traditions of spirituality, they called that honesty "humility." Now, humility is often understood as low self-esteem, though it is not. In fact, self-confidence and humility coincide when we are in touch with our center, as Jesus invites us to be.

The way to the center indeed appears to be a narrow door to those of us who have not had a good model of the spiritual life. We must not imagine, however, that the weak and confused and ill among us are at a disadvantage when it comes to entering God's house.

Recently I took our daughter Holly to have an "MRI," a Magnetic Resonance Imaging of her knee to determine whether her soccer injury was a torn ligament, cartilage damage, or something else. The patient is wheeled inside a large machine, on a cart, and the imaging is done in a powerful magnetic field.

I was asked if I wanted to be with her, and I said I did, and we both removed all our metal objects, and I sat on a chair near her head as they moved her into the machine. Within the first two minutes, I felt a weird pulling sensation in my upper body and face. I didn't know the cause, but I knew I couldn't take thirty to forty minutes of that pressure. My heart was beating fast, and I didn't know whether it was my own anxiety, or thin boundaries empathizing with what I assumed Holly would be feeling, or if I was feeling actual vibrations. All I knew was that I could not stay there for thirty minutes. I signaled the technician, and she let me out. So much for "Super Mom" sitting at her daughter's side, imparting the peace of God! I was preoccupied with "What's happening to *me?*"

I waited in the lobby, reflecting on all the years before I got into this "feeling" stuff—how rock-like I used to be, sitting at people's bedsides as they died, watching autopsies performed, with all my feelings tucked neatly away in some secret, tightly sealed compartment.

Holly came out, and she was fine. Mom was not doing so well. Any *real* Mom, and, for sure, a *real* pastor, would not have crumbled in the crunch.

We drove down to the hospital to have the images interpreted, and there we ran into the chaplain, with whom I had worked in the Clinical Pastoral Education program and whom I know as a beautiful spirit and a man of strong faith. I told him about the MRI and my own fears and reactions to it. He said, "Oh, I had to have a CAT scan once, where they put you inside the machine. It was awful; I got claustrophobic. I thought, 'My God, if I have a problem, no one can hear me!' I was scared to death! 'What's going to happen to me now?' "

I could feel my whole body relax as this chaplain, in the sharing of his own fear and anxiety and "faithlessness," gave me permission to accept and embrace my fear and anxiety and "faithlessness." I had been sure I was the only one afraid. He permitted me to feel, to let out my secrets, to become real. It was a place that felt like home, in the best sense of the word. It was later that evening that I realized none of us had considered my wire-rim glasses a "metal object."

Although the way to the center is a narrow door, the weak and ill and confused among us are at no disadvantage when it comes to entering God's house. Jesus himself waits by the door for each of us. When we are aware of our need, we will find our way to him.

God's house is open to all: male and female, gay and straight, poor and rich, homeless and middle-class, black and white. Bag ladies, children of welfare hotels, homosexuals, the mentally and physically handicapped are among those who shall come from the east and west, the north and south, to take their places at God's great feast. God will anoint and elect into service those whom some consider morally inferior, physically defective, or spiritually lost.[3] All that has been lost can be found!

It is a twilight journey through the narrow door, a winding road to sacred ground, where we take off our shoes, in awe, as we discover that all that we've lost can be found! Yes, all that we've lost will be found.

TWILIGHT JOURNEY—A SONG OF RECOVERY
by Robert Baker

Accompanied by bears with velveteen ears, the winding road journey of twilight and tears,
Extending a hand, more frightened than brave, and each of us sure we're the only one afraid,
We stand arm in arm, a circle made one, inviting our silent hearts' stories be sung,
Trying first steps, permission to feel, and letting out secrets, our souls become Real,
And there's something about the shape of these trees and the shimmering stars and the feel of this breeze; I remember this road from so long ago; and I feel like I'm on my way home.
Yes, I feel like I'm on my way home.

From love given freely and gently and true, now something feels stronger and something feels new.
From a lost band of strangers, a family we've made, and we started so different to end up the same.
There's something about the shape of these trees, and the shimmering stars, and the feel of this breeze; I remember this road from so long ago; and I feel like I'm on my way home.
Yes, I feel like I'm on my way home.

Oh, twilight journey to sacred ground, we leave our shoes on the ground,

Oh, twilight journey to an ancient town, where all that we've lost can be found.
And all that we've lost *can be* found!
Yes, all that we've lost will be found.

And all that we've lost will be found. Yes, all that we've lost will be found.
Yes, I do believe that all that we've lost will be found.
Yeah, Yeah, all that we've lost will be found.

Suggestions for Prayer or Journaling:

1. In what areas of your life do you have the most difficult time letting go and letting God? What exactly is it that you are hanging onto?

2. Do you see a *pattern* in what it is that causes you to lose confidence in your center and to look for yourself in addictions to which you give your energies? What is the pattern?

3. Go to a library and check out a record of sacred music in a language you do not know (French, German, Latin, etc.). Lie down on the floor and listen to it, letting it wash over you without the necessity of having to "understand" it.

STEP 8

We make a list of all persons we have harmed, and become willing to make amends to them all.

I Am Enough

The passage from the gospel of Mark is clearly describing the carrying of this message to others, but as I reflected on it, I realized the importance for us also of Paul's words to the people in Ephesus. The place where the two texts come together is the eighth step, where we consider that, before we can carry the message out to others, perhaps we have to carry it to ourselves.

The journaling workbook *The Twelve Steps: A Way Out* suggests that when we sit down to make a list of all persons we have harmed, we may discover that the person we have harmed most is ourself. That is, through the typical co-dependent characteristics of thinking we have to do it all, and do it perfectly as well, we set ourselves up for excessive self-blame, guilt, and shame which eventually spirals downward into an internal message that we send ourselves, that says not "I *made* a mistake," but "I *am* a mistake." The over-responsibility we grew accustomed to taking—responsibility for everybody and everything, which is, of course, an impossibility—eventually negates our very personhood and dignity as children of God, chosen in Christ, before the foundation of the world, holy and blameless before God according to the purpose of God's will.

This expresses itself in a kind of "pardon me for living!" mentality that we carry with us into adulthood. A friend of mine still laughs about her response to a neighbor a few years ago who complained that my friend's house blocked the sun from getting to her kitchen plants. My friend—not very in touch with issues of co-dependency at the time—apologized to the woman for blocking her sunshine! To this day we laugh about that—probably because it's not funny!

One person shared with a journaling workshop group precisely the essence of the text from Ephesians, and she gave me permission to share parts of it in a homily I preached on this. She had just

returned from her high school class reunion where she had experienced the kind of spiritual awakening that the Twelfth Step refers
to. That is, she experienced being totally and unconditionally accepted just as she is now—"as-is, in-process." As a result of that
experience, she came home and wrote a letter of amends to herself.
It took an almost poetic shape, and is called "I Am Enough." It goes
something like this:

> I am enough, just as I am,
> Just fine, complete, and whole—
> Satisfactory, just as I am.
> I've been covering up a hole that didn't exist,
> Achieving, achieving, when I'm already enough!
> There is no hole to fill, I am whole already. . . .
> Then I am holy!

There we have the essence of Paul's introduction to the letter to
the Ephesians. It is this kind of "spiritual awakening" that the
Twelfth Step describes as being necessary before we can carry the
message out to others. It is to know that "I am enough." But what
does that mean?

I think it means that being holy isn't a matter of what we do,
but who we are before God. To live behaviorally appropriate and
morally impeccable lives may have been what we've thought—or
were taught—that holiness means, but holiness must consist in
something other than our behavior and our "deserving" it, if God
declared us holy and blameless before the foundation of the world.
The key to this kind of understanding is the phrase "in Christ."

A woman wrote me a few weeks ago asking for some clarity
about what that means. She was confused because what she heard
and what she saw going on at her church were so different; the
mixed messages were a problem for her. She wrote: "Everyone at
this church is into 'doing' not 'being.' I'm trying to learn about
'being.' I have to 'be' before I can 'do.' Does Jesus understand?"

Yes, Jesus understands! That was the whole point of his coming! And even though the woman writing to me didn't realize it yet,
she understands too—intuitively at this point, though not cogni-
tively. Paradoxically, confusion is the gateway—the toll booth, if
you like—to understanding and enlightenment.

I was reading an article by an eastern spiritual writer as I tried to discern whether to keep or discard the book catalogue I received from his publisher, and I was struck by the way in which his own spiritual experience outside of traditional western religion paralleled very closely this text from Ephesians. He said that at the time of his own spiritual awakening, he saw that we are, at any moment, always and already free. He knew that he was not lacking anything he needed yet to find, nor had he ever been without such a thing. He is always already free. What happened for him is that he came to intuit the prior condition of freedom that is our given state.

In this gospel lesson, Jesus tells the disciples to go on their journey just as they are. "He charged them to take nothing for their journey except a walking stick; no bread, no bag, no money in their belts," not even an extra shirt. In the parallel account of this lesson in the books of Matthew (chapter 10) and Luke (chapter 9), the disciples are instructed not to even take a walking stick. Jesus simply sends them out to be together in small groups, trusting that God will provide for their needs along the way. They are enough.

That means that ministry is not a private and individual thing; it is a public and corporate vocation carried out in community. Wherever two or three are gathered together in Christ, there is authority which expresses itself in power which casts out evil. But this power is the power of God, which, paradoxically, is made perfect in our weakness. And that is the only kind of "perfection" the authentic spiritual life promises. Because ministry to others—what we call the Twelfth Step—is not a human possibility. It is possible only in dependence upon God. All that is necessary is for us to shed our illusions of self-sufficiency and independence so that the transcendent power of God can direct us and sustain us in our outreach to others.

"I am enough" not because I am "perfect" and have it all together, but "I am enough" because God has decided I am enough. In the Old Testament, when Moses asks what God's name is, God replies, "I AM. Tell them 'I AM' has sent you." So it is "I AM" who does the doing in us, and "I AM" who is enough!

How does all this operate in real life out on the sidewalk? Two illustrations came to me: one about how our inadequacies serve God's purposes, and one about ministry as an experience of community.

This week I recalled a letter I received after a Cursillo renewal weekend where I had led the music. The letter was the beginning of

a long-time friendship I've had with a woman who is now an Epis-
copal priest. It was her letter, which I've kept with my music since
that weekend, that taught me the meaning of "I am enough."

On that weekend I had wanted to do the Jesuits' song "Like a
Shepherd" on Saturday night in chapel. It's a really prayerful setting
right before bed, and the song is a very gentle portrayal of God's love
as like that of a shepherd holding the lambs carefully in his arms,
close to his heart. But there's this C-sharp chord in it which I can
never find in a hurry, much less in the dark, and when I hit whatever
other chord it was I found instead, it was so horrible even I stopped
singing. I felt like, "Well, so much for that song!" It was such a break
in the mood! I guess I picked it back up somewhere and finished
it—I don't really remember. But the following week I received this
letter from another member of the leadership team who was struggling with a call to ministry but feeling she could never be
"enough." The letter says, in part:

> The chord that was difficult—the slip of your voice—
> taught me something very important. What it showed me
> was that, despite our mistakes, faults, and failures, the love
> of others and of God which pushes us to be shepherds is far
> more important than what we actually do. The love, the
> desire to serve, the desire to comfort in your voice were
> communicated in a very special way to me. I will never
> hear that song again or read the Twenty-Third Psalm
> without remembering that being a shepherd means only
> to love and to want to give comfort and direction, without
> worrying about my abilities or my failures. Somehow,
> God takes our desire to be loving and perfects it into a
> suitable instrument for God's plans.

What the letter said to me, then and again recently, was: I am
enough—just as I am.

The second illustration came to me as I was trying to figure out
how to facilitate small-group work in my congregation. I really do
believe small groups are the life-blood of the church. I grew up in a
4,000-member church where small groups were the only way you
ever got to really know people, and such groups truly were the way
of the early church as well. But as I pondered the number of hours in
a week, and considered the number of other opportunities we're

organizing and offering, it was clear that, while I can get them started and provide some initial spiritual direction, the groups will have to have, by necessity, their own direction that comes from being gathered together in Christ. The direction will be there by the power of the Spirit. We don't have to understand how that is.

The point is: You are enough. I am enough. We are enough. Just as we are. Because God is enough. Praise to God's name. We are made for the praise of God's glorious name. God chose us to be those who trust in God's ways—those who trust in God's ways. So be it.

Suggestions for Prayer or Journaling:

1. In what area of your life do you feel you need to be "more"? Let God speak to you in the silence about this area. Write what you hear.

2. Recall a situation where you were sure you had "messed" up but later someone told you how helpful/meaningful your presence or actions were to him or her. How did you feel? How do you feel now?

In God's House Are Many Rooms

Read and reflect: John 14:1–14; 1 Peter 2:2–10

The lesson from the first letter of Peter lays the groundwork for the important message in the gospel of John. Peter reminds us that we "grow up" to salvation. Salvation is not an event, but a process. Understanding salvation in that way, as process, keeps us from interpreting this gospel text in narrow ways that have been used in the church to make Jesus' message one of exclusion rather than inclusion. When the words of John are read as prescriptive rather than descriptive of the Christian life, "belief" becomes the next "hoop" through which we have to jump in order to be okay.

The phrase "No one comes to God but by me" has often been interpreted in a very narrow way to imply that unless and until we have our doctrine and "belief" all neatly worked out, we are "lost." I think that is one of the most destructive teachings in the Christian church today. My prayer is that these reflections on the text may be a small step toward making amends to those, including ourselves, whom the church has excluded with such a narrow interpretation of this scripture.

"Life as a follower of Christ is a mystery. . . . The meaning of the word 'mystery' implies that while never totally comprehensible, the reality in question is intelligible and cries out to be pondered."[1] What is essential is not intellectual assent to some doctrine about Jesus, but rather a relationship of trust in Jesus. But such a relationship "is not valued through conceptual understanding but through the 'inner-standing' of experience. . . . Faith is what encompasses us so that we are protected in fearful situations."[2]

Jesus is the "way, the truth, and the life," but what does it mean to assert that no one comes to God but by Jesus? It gives me great comfort to read in this text that even the closest followers of Jesus, those who were present with him in history, couldn't "get it right" either. Philip—after Jesus has just told him that knowing Jesus is knowing God—asks Jesus, "Show us God." Jesus, kind of exasperated, replies, "Have I been with you so long, and yet you do not know me, Philip?" Philip needs to hear it again another way, apparently.

Well, I can relate to that! Some of us take the long way around, and if we need scriptural validation for that, here it is: the Bible says there are many rooms in God's house and a place is prepared there for us. That means that we are and can be individuals, not puppets. We just need to trust that. How do we come to that kind of trust? Through our life experience of not being discarded or abandoned just because we are "lost." We don't have to "believe" in umbrellas to experience dryness under one. I think that the way God works is that we are first brought out of the rain, and then we look up and say, "What is this? Oh, an umbrella!"

In my own life, I went through a ten year period where I didn't "believe" in anything. I called myself an atheist (quite proudly) and then changed that gradually to "agnostic" as I conceded that perhaps I did not have the corner on ultimate truth.

During my "atheist" period, when I could hardly have been said to be conformed to orthodox Christian belief, I was putting myself through college on loans and scholarships. In my sophomore year, when money was running out, I got a call from a man about a job I'd been too proud to even apply for. I wouldn't have called that "grace" at the time, or attributed it to God, because I didn't believe in God. But, fortunately, God's grace is not a prisoner of my belief.

In my junior year, I got a scholarship from a woman's club which was primarily a Jewish organization. By this time I believed something, but I didn't know what. Officially, of course, by baptism, I was still a Christian, but if so, I couldn't figure out why a Jewish group I didn't even know would give me money for college. It was one of those "mysteries" I finally had to let go of. What I was experiencing was being cared for despite my belief, or lack of it— God's unconditional love. I can look back now and see that what Jesus was in his life, ministry, and death was the incarnation of God's undying love for us. But at the time I didn't—and couldn't— "believe." Fortunately, in God's house there are many rooms, and so a place for the confused.

What years of therapy and recovery later taught me is that my "unbelief" was really anger at God. My mother had been mugged and beaten badly when I was in the eighth grade, and I was so angry at a God who would allow that injustice that the only "power" I had was to withhold my belief. Fortunately, God was not a prisoner of my anger.

Many years later, one of the ways, paradoxically, that I came back to the Christian faith was through my reading of the eastern religions. I became able to see in eastern writings and meditation the meaning of the Christian scriptures. I felt a closer affinity to eastern and Jewish mystics than I did to many conservative Christian writers.

One day in seminary, we had a "cluster" day, where all three seminaries in our cluster get together and share a day of worship, prayer, and study. I chose a workshop on contemplative prayer and was excited to see gathered there many of the faculty whom I respected at the seminary to which I had just transferred. I looked around the table and saw my own advisor, who was the professor of worship and was writing a book on prayer; the professor of the course on the sacraments who also teaches about the stages of faith; the professor who teaches spirituality and Christian education; and the head of the alcohol and drug abuse ministry program at the seminary. Also present was the academic dean of the host seminary and a few other faculty—not too many students. I decided to just listen, and eventually, the conversation turned to the subject of eastern religions and Theravadan Buddhism, a form of Buddhism stressing the original monastic discipline and the attainment of enlightenment by meditation.

The dean had real problems with this, and said, very honestly, "I don't know about Theravadan Buddhism; all I know is the God of the gospels. All I can understand is the God of the gospels." I waited for the faculty I knew to explain how the eastern and western traditions interface at the level of deep prayer, but no one said anything. Finally, I couldn't stand it—that a seminary dean would have so narrow a view of prayer and union—and I blurted out in frustration, "But it is precisely the God of the gospels who explodes all our narrow constructs about a God who cannot meet people in Theravadan Buddhism!"

The dean looked at me as if I was from Mars. Total non-comprehension of my words. And then I learned what I hadn't come to learn. Then I understood the wisdom of the other members' silence, and I knew more fully what it means that "in God's house there are many rooms." My faculty friends didn't need to change or convert this man. They were respecting where he was and letting him be there. They knew that God is not a prisoner of our belief. I discovered *I* wasn't so sure yet!

We're all in-process along the way to deeper faith and understanding. Recently I had lunch with a pastor from a denomination which makes my theology and beliefs seem conservative and narrow by comparison. He said he got in trouble once for trying to serve eucharist in his Sunday morning worship service. I asked why; what was the resistance? He said, "Too many memories for people, destructive experiences around communion in their churches when they were growing up, not being 'good enough,' being refused communion when they were divorced, many reasons." His whole congregation has rejected much of what we celebrate as Christian tradition and teaching. But as I listened, I discerned that much of what is there is not "unbelief" so much as anger, and I recalled the experience of my own journey. Fortunately, God is not a prisoner of our anger.

When our family returned home after the ecumenical community Good Friday service this year, my son had some questions about the service. He wanted to know why they would presume to pray for people who "don't know Christ," as if that is a judgment we can make from the outside. I was very taken with the theological depth of his question. It is quite true, after all, that if we really wish to probe the meaning of "belief" as *trust,* then those who don't "believe in Christ" are very likely sitting next to us in church on Sunday! People like Thomas and Philip in this passage from John's gospel are just more honest about owning that.

To be "in Christ" is not to be at a particular place on the credal or doctrinal spectrum of belief. Rather,

> In Christ shall true hearts everywhere their high communion find;
> in . . . Christ there is no East or West, in Christ no South or North,
> but one great fellowship of love throughout the whole wide earth.

"Love can exclude no race or creed if honored be God's name; our common life embraces all whose Maker is the same."[3] Truly, in God's house are many rooms.

Suggestions for Prayer or Journaling:

1. Close your eyes and picture the "house" of God. What is your "room" like? Who is there? What is the way there?

2. Make a list of people, including yourself if appropriate, whom your belief system has excluded as recipients of God's love in Christ. What needs to happen for you to become willing to make amends to them?

STEP 9

We make direct amends to such people wherever possible, except when to do so would injure them or others.

Rhythms of Life

Read and reflect: Mark 6:30–34; Ephesians 2:11–22

Having considered, in looking at the eighth step, that perhaps the person we had harmed most was ourself, with all the striving to achieve, achieve, achieve, we discovered that we're already there—we're already "enough." Here, then, I want to take that same theme the next step. So, what do we do about that realization? I think we have to get in touch first of all with exactly where it is that we are, and then it's easier to know what to do about it.

Last week I went out after dinner to play tennis with my son, Kevin, our twelve year old. I haven't even picked up a racquet for years, and it's been twenty-five years since I really took a course with score keeping and all that. So, unconsciously, I resumed playing the game right where I left off in my development as an eighteen year old—running all over the place, trying to hit balls eight feet above my head or outside the lines. Somewhere along the way, I noticed Kevin over there across the court, cool as a cucumber, swinging only at things within the small squares and letting everything out of bounds and high *be* out of bounds and high. I'm running all over the place, and he's over there just calling out the score as the balls sail over, "Deuce! . . . My ad! . . . Game!"

Finally—being a quick learner, or getting tired—I caught on and saw the larger symbolism in the whole thing. Trying to "do" life outside of reasonable boundaries is a frustrating and exhausting experience. Even Kevin got tired eventually, so obviously there are limits to our endurance even within the boundaries. When I paid attention to what was going on and adjusted my expectations to what was realistic, the game improved greatly, and in the end we tied!

So, the first important thing is to start tuning in to what's going on here, what we're doing—to know when we're trying to do too much. Jesus says to the apostles in today's gospel lesson: "Come away by yourselves and rest awhile!" That's easier said than done, and if you read on into the text, you notice that the disciples never got there! I know I, for one, have a very high energy level, and I can get completely out of touch with my body very easily if I don't pay attention to it.

One night I lay down when I got home at 6 P.M. to rest, and it was nine o'clock before I had the energy to go downstairs to make a sandwich for dinner, and I couldn't figure out what I'd done that day that was particularly draining. And right there, I think, is the problem. We don't have to figure our bodies out, we just have to listen to them. The next morning, coincidentally, I happened to look at the list of subliminal affirmations I have been playing this month. I had read them at the beginning of the month, and then forgotten what exactly these messages coming in to my unconscious were, so I looked them up again. One of the statements was: "I rest when I am tired."

I am firmly convinced that our love for others is directly related to our stress level. It just seems so obvious to me, not only from Jesus' example, urging his disciples to rest, but from all of our own life's experiences. One year I noticed that every time I went to Florida by myself for a "sabbatical," I seemed to have infinite patience down there, with little irritations like other drivers cutting in front of me, and long lines in the grocery stores. I am Ms. Mellow Person down there, but what I realized was that it is because in that environment, at that time, I am my only responsibility. There is no family to care for, no rent to pay, no orthodontist, no veterinarian, only myself. The stress level is non-existent for me on Sanibel Island.

I think all of us have become aware that the tendency to dysfunction increases as our relationships multiply and we have less energy available to listen, to care, and to feel with the other. And that is true both in families and in organizations, whether it's where you work or in your own congregation. Pope John XXIII said that, as part of his personal rule for his own prayer life, he set apart special time for recreation and sleep.

So we need space and time away to rest. There are rhythms of life, just as there are rhythms in music. In music, as Peggy Moon notes in an article in *Weavings,* "Even the long periods of rest between notes are important, for then when we are heard again, the freshness of a new voice adds richer quality to the whole."[1] We enter in, then we rest, we enter back in, and we rest again.

Another United Methodist pastor called me one day in 1988 to tell me he had contacted Marion Woodman—a Jungian analyst who writes on addictions as a paradigm for idolatry in general—and that he couldn't get her to come until 1991, because 1989 was to be her "resting" year. She's going "out"—or "in," depending on how you look at it. Jungian analysts are very sensitive to the natural rhythms of body, soul, and spirit, so that they are attuned to the life flowing from within them.

Peggy Moon continues, "The flowing from within me [is] that unique part written for me alone by the Master Composer. And I need to perceive that the rhythms of my life fit into the rhythms of the lives around me, before me, and after me, participating with them in creating the timeless masterpiece of God's symphony. . . . The rhythms of our lives comprise the symphony of God's creation —a work which has been in progress longer than any other."[2] What counts most is that we are members of that orchestra.

One night early in my ministry when our Pastor-Parish Relations Committee met, one thing that wasn't on our "agenda" was that I got in touch there with some feelings of being overwhelmed with how much there is to beginning a new ministry. It was clear to all of us, if not before that night, that I can't do this all myself, and if I try and burn out, there won't be a Twelve Step church, because— at least at early stages of things for the first few years—no one else really knows what we're doing here. We're just finding that out ourselves! Together we are all creating this ministry, God and us . . . mainly God. And I don't plan to go through burnout; I already did that once.

So the chair announced one Sunday that we would need people to serve on some committees we drew up, but it works like this. You know the poster of Uncle Sam with his finger pointing out and the words, "Uncle Sam wants you"? Well, I saw that poster a lot of years, but I never was in the army. The army wasn't part of the rhythm of my particular life. In other words, some people who are entering a resting phase will need to say "no" to committee involvement. Others, who may be just leaving their resting phase, may be willing to work on something here—but perhaps we didn't know them if they are new or have been in "hibernation." So those people may need to come and ask, "What can I do to help here?" The point is, the work will get done. We just need to be sensitive to our own rhythm and know when to say "yes" or feel free to say "no." It is certainly true that we have to choose where, among all the places in life, to put our time. Choosing to put it into the Twelve Step church has meant, for me, that I have had to let go of some other things. There are some choices we make, but we are not victims. I chose to put my time into developing co-dependency meetings here at this church because I hope to create something here that will serve needs not being met yet in other places. So it's a trade-off. And service is always a choice.

To those who are entering their "resting" phase and need to pull back, we need to remember that ministry—Twelfth Step work, we would call it—still goes on, even in the retreat phase. As I reflected on that this week, I realized that every article I have had published has been written down at the beach or somewhere on retreat. The first one was actually a letter back to my spiritual director, and it was on that particular time away that I had my most profound "Aha!" experience about the place of suffering in our lives.[3]

So, rather than being time "wasted," it is precisely our "R & R" time that renews us for creative new ministry to others. There is no running away. Not only lonely and hurting people but even little animals we stumble across on the beach remind us of that. The truth itself is what, sooner or later, calls us back. The question is not, as some of the mystics have argued over the years, whether we have to choose between being "active" or "contemplative." It's not either/or; it's both/and, a rhythm of life. There is always the tension between rest and work, being and doing. The important thing is to get the order in order. Our doing must first come out of our being. We never serve—"do"—in order to be accepted or loved. We are loved, and out of that joy we are freed to offer our service. That is the difference between law and gospel, and precisely what Paul is talking about in his letter to the Ephesians, where he says that Christ has broken down the dividing wall of hostility by abolishing the law of commandments and ordinances, so making peace and reconciling us both to God and to each other, and thereby bringing hostility to an end. If we understand that much right there, we have the entire New Testament message in a nutshell.

How do we tell if our priorities are in order? My own index for myself is that if I start resenting my service, then I know my order is getting reversed. More love is going out than is coming in. Then I need to pull back and say "Whoa"—time to receive, first, because you can't pour out of an empty cup.

The work at church, in your home, or in your office will get done. God takes care of that somehow. I seldom preach "Serve," "Give," or "Do." But when we have needs, all those needs get met.

One thing I read in the journaling workbook *The 12 Steps—A Way Out* surprised me. It didn't surprise me that it's true, but that I found it in a secular co-dependency journal. It said about the Ninth Step: "The readiness to accept the full consequences of our past, and, at the same time, take responsibility for the well-being of others, is the very spirit of step nine." I think that often, in the program, we begin to think that any kind of caring for others' needs is "caretaking" and co-dependence, and that belief can lead to real problems in a Christian community. Caring for others is not co-dependent. We are all in this life together.

Some years ago I went through burnout and just absolutely hit bottom. There's a cartoon I have that pictures what that is like: there is a pile of ashes beside the pulpit with smoke rising from it. At that time I walked into church one day with hardly the strength to sing, and the pastor just happened to have chosen this song. Tears came down as I read the words of love that this God, who will not let us go, has for us:

O love, that wilt not let me go, I rest my weary soul in thee;
I give thee back the life I owe, that in thine ocean depths its
  flow may richer, fuller be.

O Light that followest all my way, I yield my flickering torch
  to thee;
My heart restores its borrowed ray, that in Thy sunshine's blaze
Its day may brighter, fairer be.

O Joy that seekest me through pain, I cannot close my heart
    to thee;
I trace the rainbow through the rain, and feel the promise is
    not vain
That morn shall tearless be.

So be it!

Suggestions for Prayer or Journaling:

1. Are you in a resting phase now? What is your attitude toward service/work for others? Do you feel resentment?

2. Reflect back to the last "R & R" you had. How long ago was it? What shape did it take? Were you surprised to find new ministry/growth coming directly out of it?

3. Schedule an appointment for a full body massage as part of your "R & R." Many retreat centers, offering spiritual direction, now offer massage also.

And Who Is My Neighbor?

Read and reflect: Luke 10:25–37; Colossians 1:1–14

No matter how unacquainted we are with the Bible, this story is probably not new to us. The secular world has appropriated the story. Just this week in a movie we were watching, one character exclaimed to the other, "Well, aren't you the good Samaritan!" But secular appropriations of the story usually miss the deeper meanings that are hidden within the biblical text and which require some understanding of the Christian tradition and scriptures.

First of all, the fact that the priest and Levite pass by the injured person needs to be "fleshed out." Leviticus 22, which contains the biblical regulations concerning priests, instructs religious leaders that if they have contact with a dead body, they become ritually unclean (Lev 22:4–7). So for a priest and Levite—the Levite would be the "assistant" in our language—to avoid contact with what appeared to be a corpse would be a matter of obedience to what they thought was the divine will. To "pass by on the other side" would be what, to their understanding, they were supposed to do in order to be "clean" to offer the holy gifts at worship. An analogy that came to me as I tried to think of a way to explain this (but analogies always break down) would be if, on a communion Sunday, one of the kids during the children's moment had an "accident"; would it be prudent for me to clean it up and then still break the bread and serve it?

Second, it's important to have a sense of the degree of the depth of hostility between the people of Samaria and the Jews in order to experience the same surprise and offense the ancient listeners would have had when a Samaritan comes out as "hero" in this story. Differences between the Jews and the Samaritans were religious and cultural, and resulted in the two groups despising each other. The equivalent in our society would probably be like the emotion that currently surrounds AIDS. Anyone not like the Jews was regarded as different, strange, almost diseased.

And here in this story we have the reversal of roles that occurs with the in-breaking of the reign of God. In the parable, wounded-ness becomes a source of healing power. And now there is some "meat" in the reading of the passage. That is, the parable's purpose is not to judge the behavior of the priest and the Levite, who in various ways were within the law of their time, but to make a claim on the truer and deeper spiritual law alive in ordinary life. Often, in life, we are blinded by our presuppositions, and one of the most blinding presuppositions is that God is only with us in our experi-ences of power, independence, success, and triumph. That is a kind of practical atheism because it leads us to believe that eternal life is the result of specific human behaviors we perform. And that means that, if we live long enough, we're going to have to deny a whole range of experience—the experience of lying, with the injured man, in the ditch by the side of the road.

The first message we need to receive in this passage, then, is that God is in the ditch! We are asked to see the world as the place of divine activity, which is evident daily in the individual actions of ordinary people, and most conspicuous in the unexpected actions of unexpected people. The text is about God and God's action in our lives when we're in the ditch. God is in the ditch so that we can know that we don't have to climb out of the ditch to get to God. This is far from the usual interpretation that says the reason we're in the ditch is because we're not where we need to be. In fact, we're in the ditch because we're "dead" and that is whom God deals with and is about. "We live in the garbage. Smell the garbage as the incense that rises up to heaven, rejoice in the garbage; it's the only place we're ever going to be!"[4]

Now that is not exactly my hope for "eternal life," but what Bogie means is that recovery involves coming to terms with our past, and if we have in our past that which we cannot accept or look at, then our recovery is blocked. In our recovery, we will be shown parts of ourselves that are the wounded half-dead traveler, parts that are the priest and Levite trying to "get it right and be perfect," and parts that are the good Samaritan. Wholeness means coming to terms with all of those parts of ourselves, though not becoming identified with any one of them.

We are shown our own suffering as the place where we have been in God's presence. The Samaritan remembered what it was like to be lying by the side of the road. The text says that the Samaritan "felt compassion." In Latin the word "compassion" means "to suffer with," that is, to remember enough of your own suffering so that you share in the suffering of another. Maybe the Samaritan remembered what it is like to be wounded. People who've been in the ditch can recover their ditch experience and then become bearers of this mercy for others.

But the story doesn't stop there. What defines hospitality or neighborliness is action, not words alone. The sentence goes on without break: "And when he saw him, he felt compassion, and came to him, and bandaged up his wounds, pouring oil and wine on them; and he put him on his own beast, and brought him to an inn, and took care of him." The Samaritan took care of the wounded person.

And right here is where I see an incredibly important message for us on our own journey as ACOAs. Carl Jung said, in talking to a group of pastors in 1932:

> What if I should discover that the poorest of all beggars, the least of all my brethren—these are within me, and that I myself stand in the need of the alms of my own kindness, that I myself am the enemy who must be loved—what then?

The Hazelden book, *Stairway to Serenity: The Eleventh Step,* goes on to ask, "Is it possible that we despise some people because they are as unworthy and unattractive as we imagine ourselves to be? Is it possible that we fear others because we suspect they are too much like the worst in ourselves—critical, vindictive, uncompromising and unforgiving?"[5]

To have mercy on, to take care of, the wounded person within is perhaps the most important work that is set before us, because to love our neighbor as ourself presupposes a self that has been cared for. What is needed is, as for the Samaritan, awareness of the injury, and then some intentionality and follow-through about caring for the wounds. "To make amends" is not to stop at being sorry or wishing things had been different. To make amends is to make changes that alter our current reality—changes in our attitudes and in our behaviors toward, first of all, ourselves.

I experienced this in my own life as I was waiting for my son

Aaron at his swimming lesson. One day I noticed a father playing with his two year old daughter as they waited for the brother's lesson to be over. Dad wasn't just "killing time," though; he was attending to her, playing games with her, talking to her, caring for her. Tears came as I experienced the loss of that kind of interaction in my own childhood. The next day I saw them again and I felt more "neutral." I had cried those tears and felt a strange kind of happiness for her, this child today who is getting her needs met. I didn't understand that, but I am really trying these days to just let be whatever is. The third day, an interesting transition took place: as I watched Dad put her on his shoulders and carry her around, it was I who was on his shoulders enjoying the ride. We were one family. We were one. We were *one.* I told my husband later that it seemed almost like a metaphor, for me, of the process/journey in general—that first we have to own and feel the pain and loss, and grieve that, and then God moves us on to form a kind of "scab" so to speak, so that the skin becomes strong again and we can get on with life. God bandages our wounds. That incident and its healing does not mean that I am done with the loss and grief work, because I think these kinds of happenings keep coming before us all our lives. But as the healing goes on, the intensity dissipates, and we are increasingly able to use our pain in the service of others, instead of drowning in it ourselves.

The movie I mentioned earlier was *Cocoon: The Return,* a sequel to an earlier movie where three retired couples leave earth with a space crew who are returning to a distant planet where there is no illness, suffering or death. In this sequel, when they return and visit their friends and families on earth, two of the couples decide to remain here and not return, even though it results in one's death from leukemia within four days. The "bottom line" of their decision—and a very profound theological truth—was that life, eternal life, is not to be found in the freedom from suffering or pain; it is in the compassion and mercy that is born out of that pain and that attends it. The characters all learn, this time around, to use their pain in the service of others. God is in the ditch.

Though the darkness may hide some of this truth from our sight at times, so that we don't always see God's glory in the ditch, it is precisely there, on the road going down from Jerusalem to Jericho, that we encounter the holy one. Thanks be to God!

Suggestions for Prayer or Journaling:

1. Write about a "ditch" experience of your own which later provided you the opportunity to be the bearer of mercy for another.

2. In what way do you now stand in need of the alms of your own kindness? What changes do you now seek to make in your attitudes or behaviors toward yourself?

STEP 10

We continue to take personal inventory and, when we are wrong, promptly admit it.

Peace Be with You

Read and reflect: John 20:19–31; 1 John 1:5–10

This reflection evolved while I sat in the dentist's chair, trying to understand why I had felt increasingly alienated from my dentist during the last several visits. This time I was very short with him, and when he asked "How are you?" I said, "Pretty irritable, actually!"

"Is the tooth bothering you?" he asked.

"No," I said. "All these trips back here are bothering me." And then, of course, there was a long twenty minute silence. And that's when I figured out both what's been going on with me and my dentist, and the meaning of these scripture texts.

The dentist has been reworking a crown on which he made an error last year about this time, and all the return trips have been to remake, refit, and reset it. I surely understand mistakes, and I do believe in the grace that covers them. But what I finally realized was bothering me was not the mistake he made. What has alienated me is the fact that he never admitted the error or apologized for my inconvenience in all these return trips to correct the problem.

As I sat there trying to get in touch with my feelings, I realized that all I really wanted was some honesty about the whole thing. Something like, "I'm really sorry. I know my mistake has caused you a lot of inconvenience." That would be the end of it, as far as I am concerned. But reconciliation presupposes the admission of error first, and an apology cannot be accepted if it is not offered.

Recently, I talked with my dad, and we had a good two-hour visit during which a lot of old family history surfaced. At one point, something came up that had happened when I was eight years old, and we talked about it now as adults. I told him that the incident, a practical joke that had humiliated me, had hurt a lot and has continued to affect my ability to trust. When he heard that, his face changed immediately, and he said, "I'm sorry; that was really uncalled for, and I'm not proud of it." *Instantly,* it was as if a fog had lifted from our whole relationship. As I was driving home, I thought, "I have been carrying that incident around for thirty-five years, and all that needed to happen was what just has: a simple acknowledgement of accountability and an apology." And *zap,* it was resolved.

One important place where the scriptures and the Twelve Step program intersect is in the understanding of what causes and what heals alienation in relationships. If we say, or think, we have no character defects, that we do not screw up, that we do not betray people, that we have no problems trusting, then we deceive ourselves, and we remain in denial. But if we acknowledge and admit these things, then God, and the people we have offended, are quick to forgive. Admission of sin, error, mistrust or whatever it is makes us very vulnerable, and vulnerability is disarming to the other.

Whenever I ask my kids "Who did such-and-such?" and one of them just says, "I did," even with no explanation or excuse, that is usually the end of the discussion. That admission disarms me and gives me just enough time to kick into gear and realize the folly of my question—the fact that, "Of course, they did such-and-such; they're kids!" But if I get denial in return, invariably it turns into a long hassle that wears all of us out.

Carl Jung, in his volume on psychotherapy, says, "Anything concealed is a secret. The possession of secrets acts like a psychic poison that alienates their possessor from the community."[1] So this scripture text is good psychology as well as good theology.

Isn't this gospel scene a marvelous paradigm for our whole lives? When Jesus comes into the room where, out of fear, the disciples have locked themselves, he says to them, "Peace be with you." The focus of the scripture lesson is trust. Jesus wants the disciples to be at peace, and he invites them to do whatever is necessary in order for that to be their reality.

Thomas cannot believe unless he sees the nail marks in Jesus' hands and side, so Jesus invites Thomas to touch him. Then Thomas believes. Jesus accommodates our unbelief. If Thomas had faked it and pretended belief, then Jesus could not have given him the proof he needed, and Thomas would have remained in doubt. But Jesus says three times, "Peace be with you." All Thomas has to do is to be honest and admit his doubt.

In the deepening life of prayer, the crucial first issue is not faith, which is always tentative, even as it was for Moses and the prophets, but honesty. Thomas is a straight arrow. He says, "I can't believe." Such honesty is the beginning of true faith. How? Because it acknowledges our helplessness and throws us back on God alone.

It is very important in the spiritual life to learn to distinguish between what theologians call "true guilt," which is there for a reason, and "false guilt" or "neurotic guilt," which is destructive to the spirit and serves no healthy purpose. Discernment between these two kinds of guilt is offered to us in many different ways.

Last week I had several restless nights. Finally I had a dream that someone I've been very close to was hurt and angry at me. At a conscious level I could not see anything that I felt I had done wrong in our relationship, but clearly the dream revealed my error and his hurt. So I called him, and we met and worked it through. As soon as I had admitted my offense, I was able to sleep again. In Psalm 32, God says, "I will instruct you and teach you the way you should go; I will counsel you with my eye upon you." That is a promise to us!

The journey is always going on at an unconscious level, and whether we realize it or not, we are all very much involved with each other in the Christian community. That's the meaning of "one body." When I shared my dream with my friend, he asked, motioning to his chest, "Are you feeling tight here?" I asked how he knew that, and he said, "Because I feel it too." We are not uninvolved with each other in this journey. We are one body; we are all inter-connected.

Jesus breathed on the disciples and said to them, "If you forgive the sins of any, they are forgiven; if you retain the sins of any, they are retained." This is a real power we have been given over each other, and a real challenge as well, to use that power responsibly.

In Robert Baker's beautiful song "Dance With Me!" he sings, "Healing is ours to give or withhold, we ask for this power from You." It is only in the right use of this power that we will experience the peace that passes all understanding, for eternal life is partnership with God, and with one another. Peace be with you!

Suggestions for Prayer and Journaling:

1. Read and reflect on Psalm 32 this week as a morning and evening meditation.

2. Ask God to speak to you about the difference between true guilt

and false or neurotic guilt in your life. Write in your journal what you hear God speaking.

3. In what "room" of your life have you locked yourself in fear? Close your eyes and imagine yourself there and see Jesus coming into it now. He looks at you and addresses you, "Peace be with you . . ." Dialogue with him there.

Life on the Roller Coaster

Read and reflect: Luke 16:19–31; 1 Timothy 6:6–19

We were watching *48 Hours* on the night before Hurricane Hugo hit, and the whole program was about the preparations being made for the coming storm. The reporter was interviewing the chief of police of Charleston, South Carolina. He asked him if the forecasts about the time and place of the hurricane's arrival would lessen the number of casualties. "Who will die in this hurricane?" he asked. The police chief responded matter-of-factly, "Those who think it's going to affect you, but not them—only the other guy."

The reporter seemed so surprised that pinpointing the exact hour and destination of the storm would still not serve as sufficient warning. Why would people not listen to the warnings to take the necessary precautions? As I watched this program, with all the scientific weather data, charts and photos of the storm, I too had to wonder. If people wouldn't listen to the mayor's warnings, would they become convinced even if someone killed by a previous storm should rise from the dead and speak to them?

A few days later we were watching the news accounts in the aftermath of Hugo, and another reporter, interviewing a woman who had come back now to assess the damage to her home, asked the woman, "Were you able to save anything?" And without one second's hesitation, she replied, "We were able to save the kids, and that's the important thing!"

Her response captures the essence of both these New Testament texts—that life is about relationships, not about things. Paul says, in the epistle lesson, "We brought nothing into the world and we cannot take anything out of the world. . . . Aim at righteousness . . . take hold of the eternal life to which you are called. . . . If we have food and clothing, with these we shall be content."

"Righteousness" is one of those theological words that can throw us for a loop if we're not careful. It is used about six hundred

123

times in the Bible and when I looked it up in my reference book, there were twenty long pages of fine print explaining its real meaning. In a nutshell, the common misunderstanding is that "righteousness" means getting it right—some form or other of moral or ethical purity we "achieve" so that we're then OK and acceptable. And to understand righteousness in this way is the beginning of losing hold on the eternal life to which we are called!

Rather, righteousness is simply about "right relationships," and even that does not mean that we are "righteous" when we get our relationships right. Righteousness is about a life in relationship of repentance and dependence upon God, not upon the other person, to meet our needs. In Twelve Step terms it means relationships based first of all in the first three steps, and then operating in the relationships out of steps four, five, six, seven, eight, nine and ten. Let's look at what that means in real life.

Phil Donahue's show one morning was on friendship. He had three people there whose friendships had all been broken because, at first explanation, the friend—the other person not present on stage —had done some flaky or insensitive thing to them. One woman had loaned a friend a lot of money and never got it back. Another man had flown to England to ask his friend to be best man at his wedding a year ahead of time, and then the friend cancelled out twenty-four hours before the wedding.

About midway through the show, Donahue brought out the people's friends, who had agreed to appear and tell their side of the story of what had broken the relationship. And what the audience discovered, as the friends spoke, was something about the nature of the human condition and human finitude.

The man who had cancelled out on the wedding turned out to be going through serious marital problems of his own that year, and being in and out of denial about that, he was just unable to accept that his own marriage was a mess. He said he could not bring himself to admit, even to himself, much less to his friend, that he could not be anyone's best man right now.

The woman who owed the money did not ever have the amount to repay her friend. Maybe she had what we would call a spending disorder. Whatever label you want to put on it, all three people were just where they were at the time, and it wasn't a very good space to be. They weren't able to be very good friends.

This led then to a discussion of "What is a friend?" And one of the women in the audience said, "It's not approval you need in a friendship, but acceptance for who you are and support in that."

That is, we don't have to agree with people's behavior or like it, but we let them be who they are. We're all at different places along the way on this journey and it's probably not very realistic to think we're going to be able to find friends who are exactly like us, who would make exactly the same choices and responses we would in a situation. As Melody Beattie said at the first national conference on co-dependency in Arizona, "What's wrong (with us) will probably always be there in one form or another. . . . We're right where we belong in this process, and others are, too." She adds, "We will achieve more power in our lives than we ever dreamed when we stop trying to control [other people's responses and behavior]."[2]

So, once again, the matter of right relationships brings us back to square one: back to the point of beginning with ourselves. As one woman said on the news, being interviewed about reconstruction efforts after Hurricane Hugo: "You start with your own house and then help others with theirs, because we're all in this together, and life has to go on." Each of us, in relationship building and reconstruction, has to start with our own house. That's the foundation of right relationship.

In the same co-dependency workshop, Melody Beattie said, "I believe of all things we're trying to accomplish in this process called recovery, the most important is learning to love ourselves . . . learning to love ourselves so much that the good stuff gets right down into the core of us and then spills out into our lives; and I believe that the purpose of learning to love ourselves is not so that we can lock ourselves in a closet and say, 'OK, here I am, I'm just taking care of me!' It's so that we can learn to participate in healthy loving relationships so that we can, number one, love others in ways that work, and then accomplish what will probably be the greatest challenge for any of us in this room: and that's learning to let other people love us."[3]

And there, in the realm of learning to receive love, we can look to our children—or the child within—to lead us. Children just seem to naturally know what will be healthy for them. Early this summer our son Aaron had a stomachache one night when I put him to bed. He said, "Cover me with a blanket." Wondering if that was the tipoff to a fever, I asked, "Are you chilled?" It was not a cool evening. "No," he said, "but people made them for me and they make me feel better." He was referring to two or three light crocheted baby blankets people made when he was born. What he experienced in those gifts was the unconditional love that we often shower on babies. But as we get older and begin to get in people's way, that's harder to offer—and to receive!

We're more able to receive love from others when we have some sense that the love will be there even when we get in their way or disagree with them. One Sunday in a Pastor-Parish Relations Committee meeting, a man from the traditional church with whom we share space was on the opposite side of an issue from where I was and, at one point, he said, "Well, Michele, I just disagree very strongly with you on this." I didn't feel at all threatened by his comment and I took a mental step back for a few minutes to ponder why I felt quite comfortable in this conversation. Maybe it's because I'm not all that sure that my position on the subject is any more "correct" than his; but more likely I think it is because he and I sat together on a pier at our denomination's annual conference last summer and he shared with me about a relative's suicide, and we talked about dysfunctional families as part of the human condition. I just trust that our relationship transcends any particular opinions we hold on any certain issue, because our relationship is based in something greater than our own opinions.

My relationship with Bogie Dunn, my former New Testament professor and now friend, is the same way. Maybe it's because of the way I met Bogie. I was walking down the stairs with a seminary classmate as Bogie's class on the letter to the Romans had just ended. My classmate was trying to convince me I ought to sit in on it. I said, "I've already had all my Bible courses before I transferred and I don't want to hear any more of the letter to the Romans." Bogie turned out to be right behind us and interjected in his inimitable probing manner, "What's that you say?" Without judgment or condemnation, Bogie let me be where I was about the study of scripture at that time, and that acceptance was the beginning of a relationship. It not only motivated me to retake from him, without credit, courses on the texts of Mark, Romans, Luke, and Revelation, as well as a course in homiletics (the art of preaching), but it also led to a relationship that entailed many lunchtime hours of conversation about theology, christology, and the meaning of life. The relationship was not based on whether Bogie liked or agreed with my thoughts or opinions, but in something greater—that the God who loves us both will deal with and eventually inform our opinions and thoughts. That is trust! And it gives me a kind of real freedom in the relationship to know that I can be who I am and I won't be thrown away.

I think that nothing points out more clearly the need for our relationships to be based in something besides our own efforts than the movie *Parenthood,* with Steve Martin in the role of a father whose own father neglected him. He, therefore, wanted to be the perfect father to his own kids. But as you watch the movie, the finitude of the human condition is quite evident both in his own present family and in his brother's and sisters' families, despite all of the parents' efforts at trying as hard as they can to "get it right."

At one important point in the movie, when everything seems to be falling apart in his life, his wife discovers she's pregnant and they discuss the problems this fourth child can bring. "It could be like Larry!" Martin exclaims. (Larry is his brother who has a gambling addiction and now owes money to the Mafia.)

Martin's wife says, "Kids are not appliances; they don't come with guarantees. Life is messy."

"I don't *like* messy," he replies. "It's so . . . *messy!*"

Grandma enters the room at this point. Grandma is one of those unpretentious sages that we all have somewhere in our families. Grandma walks in and interjects right in the middle of this discussion, "You know, when I was nineteen, your grandpa took me on a roller coaster and I thought it was so interesting that I could be so frightened, so sick, so excited, so afraid, and so happy, all by one ride. Some people didn't like it. They just wanted to ride the merry-go-round. It only went round and round and round; it didn't go anywhere. I liked the roller coaster!"

Life on the roller coaster has its way of continuously bringing us back to dependence, for our sense of security, on the steel bar that rests right in front of us but which we often like to imagine we can do the ride quite safely without holding onto.

The roller coaster is a ride we don't control and which certainly throws us some unexpected curves. But when we take hold of the bar, we take hold of the eternal life to which we are called—the life which is life indeed.

Suggestions for Prayer or Journaling:

1. In what recent relationship have you discovered you were wrong and needed to admit it? What was the outcome? What has been the effect on your expectations of others now?

2. Journal about what is hardest for you in allowing others to love you.

STEP 11

We seek through prayer and meditation to improve our conscious contact with God, as we understand God, praying only for knowledge of God's will for us and the power to carry that out.

Come to the Water

Read and reflect: 2 Kings 5:1-15

The story of Naaman is typical of all of us. Naaman wants to be healed, and he has figured out how that will take place. He expects that God's prophet will wave a hand over him and his disease will go away. Being told to go wash in a dirty river is not exactly what he has in mind. I love Naaman's honesty: "I have my own rivers back home; if I wanted to wash in a river, I'd have washed in a clean one back there."

God's solution is both simple and unexpected: "Come to the water." The punchline is in the question asked of Naaman by his servant, "If the prophet had told you to do something difficult, you would have done it. Now why can't you just wash yourself as he said, and be cured?"

We all have our views of how God should work, haven't we? And our ways are usually a lot more involved than simply, "Come to the water." If we are honest with ourselves, we see in Naaman our own pride and arrogance. We, too, want to bring our gifts or to earn God's grace. Naaman, the powerful and wealthy, is asked to accept a gratuitous healing simply by washing himself in a river. How ordinary! How humbling! The gift he brought now fades into insignificance. Twenty thousand dollars in silver and sixty thousand dollars in gold—insignificant! He is told, simply, "Come to the water."

Jesus' response, when the disciples ask him to teach them to pray, is also a simple one. He teaches them the prayer that we call the Lord's Prayer. He begins by urging them to let God be God. That is the meaning of "Hallowed be thy name." As the prayer continues, they are told to ask that God's reign may come. We might paraphrase it, "Holy God, you be God in this and do it your way." Jesus then urges the disciples to ask, seek, and knock. "For every one who asks receives, and the one who seeks finds, and to the one who knocks it will be opened" (Lk 11:1-13).

Often we ask God for our needs to be met, but then we act in ways that block our receiving. We need to ask ourselves the honest question that Jesus asks at other places in the New Testament, "Do you want to be healed?"

I sat down one Sunday evening to relax and watch a TV program called "Have Faith," a show about three or four Roman Catholic priests and their life together. In this episode a boy of about twelve had stolen money from the church's offering plate. The priests recognized by his behavior that he was hurting and were trying to love the boy rather than condemn him. They paid his bail, and the boy asked, "What's with you guys? I steal from your offering and you bail me out." One priest replied, "We just want you to stop hurting." The boy responded, "Did it occur to you that maybe I don't want to?"

In that response we have important information about "unanswered" prayer. Prayer is not genuine unless we are honest about what we really want. If the payoff we get from hurting is somehow bigger than the payoff we anticipate from changing, we will consciously or unconsciously act in ways that block receiving the very thing for which we ask. Perhaps we want friends, or a spouse, but the fear of stepping out and allowing ourselves to be known is greater than our loneliness. In our prayers we ask for friends or a mate, but then we isolate ourselves and wonder why God doesn't answer our prayer.

Knowing how to receive is very important to our Christian faith. If we are to be willing to receive what God has for us, prayer means increasing conscious contact with ourselves. In the words of Martin Luther, "It is the nature of faith that it presumes on the grace of God. . . . Faith does not require information, knowledge, or certainty, but a free surrender and joyful bet on God's unfelt, untried, and unknown goodness."

This goodness comes in strange ways. As co-dependents, we seek validation in the form of kind words and pats on the head, but God sometimes answers prayer with conflict that appears to be destructive. On reflection, however, that conflict may be God's affirmation that I can be strong, that I do know how to deal with problems, that I can be assertive. In that experience, I discover that the validation comes from within myself, and that is the real answer to my prayer.

"We may find that our apparent wants are destructive to ourselves and not what we really desire. We may discover consequences to our desires that are opposed to what we most deeply want. But this process demands openness, honesty, and profound trust."[1]

Often in my work at the church, I notice that when a person comes in with one set of questions, all written out, God may drop a wholly different agenda on our time together as we discover what is really being sought.

The more I learn about prayer, the more I am certain that Luther was right: "Faith does not require information, knowledge, or certainty, but a free surrender and joyful bet on God's unfelt, untried, and unknown goodness."

The story is told that one Sunday morning in a mountain country in central Europe, the church bells were ringing and a man walking a mountain path came upon a shepherd boy with his father's flock of sheep. The boy was kneeling and reciting the alphabet. The man asked, "What are you doing?" The boy answered, "I'm praying." Somewhat sternly, the man said, "Praying? What kind of praying is this? Just saying letters, no words at all?" The boy replied, "I've never learned any prayers, sir. But it's Sunday morning and the bells are ringing in the valley, and I wanted to pray, and I thought, well, maybe if I just said all of the letters, God might hear them and put them together for me, and spell out what I ought to say."[2]

That is true worship. It is worship in its essence, worship at its purest and best, simply to place ourselves before God and turn it all over. "Here it is, Lord; take it and make it come together as it should; take it and spell it out for me, please."

In my own life, that turning-it-over happens when I am brought to my knees. Long before I knew anything about "prayer," while working in a new and unfamiliar large city, I took a bus one night after work to an appointment with an ophthalmologist, and I got off in the wrong part of town. Immediately I could tell that the neighborhood was very rough and that I had messed up. I had no change for the phone, and so I went to a couple of apartments to ask to use the phone to call a cab, but the residents wouldn't let me in. I started walking aimlessly as it grew dark. Just about the time I was getting really frightened, a policeman drove by, but he was heading in the opposite direction. My heart sank as he passed on by. A few minutes later he pulled up beside me and opened the door. I got in, really surprised, and asked how he knew I was lost. He said, "I don't know. Something just made me turn around. I didn't know where you belong, but I knew you don't belong here." The "something" in responses like these is the Spirit of God, who knows where we belong. That event happened during my angry-at-the-church days, but that was the night I realized that the bells ring in the inner city as well as in the mountains of central Europe.

Jesus invites us all to come to the water. Maybe we can only come to the water when our jar is empty. When our jar is full, or when we think it is, we have no motivation to make the trip to the well. Only those who thirst come to the water. Those who seek . . . come to the water. Those who have nothing . . . come to the water. Those who are weary . . . come to the water. Without money, without price . . . we come to the water. We are, all, laden. We are, all, children without might. When Naaman realizes that only in Israel and through Israel's God is healing to be found, he comes to the water, and is healed.

We ponder anew, with Augustine, "How can our souls find rest, except for the Lord?"

Come to the water!

COME TO THE WATER
by John Foley, S.J.
Copyright 1978 by John B. Foley, S.J., and NALR. Used with
permission.

O let all who thirst, let them come to the water.
And let all who have nothing, let them come to the Lord:
   without money, without price.
Why should they pay the price, except for the Lord?

And let all who seek, let them come to the water.
And let all who have nothing, let them come to the Lord:
   without money, without strife.
Why should you spend your life, except for the Lord?

And let all who toil, let them come to the water.
And let all who are weary, let them come to the Lord:
   all who labor, without rest.
How can your soul find rest, except for the Lord?

And let all the poor, let them come to the water.
Bring the ones who are laden, bring them all to the Lord:
  bring the children without might.
Easy the load and light: come to the Lord.

Suggestions for Prayer or Journaling:

1. Reflect back to a time when you wanted to give someone a gift and he or she wouldn't or couldn't accept it. How did you feel? What was the outcome?

2. From whom is it hardest for you to receive: from others? from God? from yourself?

3. Reflect on the unanswered prayers in your life. In what ways do you block receiving what you pray for? How is the "payoff" you get from hurting bigger than the "payoff" you expect to receive from changing?

4. In what area of your life do you come "empty-handed" to the water?

5. Listen to a recording of John Foley's "Come to the Water," available at most Christian bookstores as part of the St. Louis Jesuits' album *Wood Hath Hope*, North American Liturgy Resources.

To Pray Always and
Not Lose Heart

Read and reflect: Luke 18:1–8

For most of us, anthropomorphic or patriarchal images of God, especially images that set God up in our minds as any kind of "judge," do not help to build our trust. Our experience with the arbitrariness of human figures makes us reluctant to accept that such a God really is "for us." The arbitrariness of nature also pushes us to find images and metaphors for God that help us to understand the delay in answer to our prayers as the result of something besides some kind of cosmic dice toss.

The first thing we have to get at in order to understand this text is what "prayer" is. While we first, probably as children, understand prayer as talking to God, usually asking only for our needs to be met, we eventually grow into a broader understanding of prayer as communion with God, which includes listening at our end. And just as in any relationship, once we start listening as well as talking, we are brought to a deeper level which moves us beyond our own desires into a consideration of the other's.

That openness to the other, and to the other's impact upon us, creates a kind of vulnerability that may be scary but which is the essence of true prayer. The call to prayer is the call to vulnerability. Today's text calls us to persist in vulnerability.

In one of the tapes from the first national conference on co-dependency, Terry Kellogg, speaking on sexual addictions, makes some very important connections. He says that sexual addiction is

> the result of cultural misogyny which is fear and hatred not of women, but of vulnerability. Our cultural misogyny is the setup for child abuse, neglect, infant mortality. . . .

Our cultural misogyny creates a worship of power, because if you fear and hate vulnerability, you end up worshipping power. Our cultural misogyny keeps us from looking at those vulnerable aspects of ourselves, our feelings, including our sexuality and our own sexual feelings. It keeps us from having healthy children because we fear and hate their vulnerability as well. It is the cause of child abuse; it is the cause of co-dependency. I always figure [he says] that if you scratch an addict, you'll find a co-dependent; scratch a co-dependent and you'll find an abused child.[4]

This is all pretty much the same thing that Alice Miller relates in her book *For Your Own Good*.[5] And James Nelson, in his book *The Intimate Connection: Male Sexuality, Masculine Spirituality*[6] proposes a "considerable re-examination of traditional models of masculinity" as he laments the attitudes in our society toward vulnerability and the consequent problems with intimacy that we have in America. Throughout his book, vulnerability emerges over and over again as the necessary "ingredient" for the effective life of prayer. He describes this as "relational power." "Relational power understands that the capacity to absorb the influence of another without losing the self's own center is as truly a quality of strength as is the exerting of influence on another."[7]

The paradox is that "the world of the individual who can be influenced by another without losing his or her identity or freedom is larger than the world of the individual who fears being influenced."[8] This is a new kind of "power," a spiritual power. "People are enhanced by this kind of power, mystery is affirmed, interdependence is celebrated." True power, then, understands that the greatest influence often consists in being influenced, in allowing another to make the largest impact on oneself."[9]

How we get from "here" to "there," according to these seminal thinkers, may come as a surprise to us. Terry Kellogg ponders the question: "Is shame the problem? Or the solution?" "Don't get rid of your feelings," he says. "Embrace your feelings. Don't reduce your shame. Embrace your shame. Your shame is a path to your vulnerability, to intimacy, and to spirituality. Your shame is a felt sense of capacity to harm, and it's a feeling that happens when we get harmed; and in the de-briefing of how we've been harmed, we access the shame, and we find our vulnerability, and vulnerability is the path to intimacy."[10]

Now if we begin to understand "prayer" in this way, a text like our gospel lesson, about why we must persist in prayer and not be discouraged, begins to make sense at a much deeper level than we used to hear it speaking. We begin to see that our own resistance is largely what is blocking us. We realize that we don't like the role of "vulnerable widow" in this text. We don't want to be needy, knocking at God's door and totally dependent upon this Other. We are confronted with the reality that we don't really wish to "pray only for God's will for us" because we still don't really trust this God!

My own recent experience with massage therapy helped me to understand the difficulty I have in trusting God. Currently I am having some work done called "deep muscle/connective tissue massage" and "trigger point therapy" for an ankle injury that is six months old and wasn't healing properly.

When my massage therapist started working on it, she explained that, to lessen the pain, I had been putting extra pressure on lots of surrounding muscles and compensating with my other foot. Additional muscle groups were now affected and strained. She goes about healing the ankle muscles by putting "ischemic pressure" on the injured foot right at the place where it hurts most, called the "trigger point." I breathe deeply through the pain and then I can gradually feel the muscle relaxing and letting go.

I understood all this psychologically and theologically first, or I would never have been able to let her do it physically, because the pain is really quite intense, and she has radar to find those trigger points. She will press down and ask if "this is where it hurts." Many times I've felt like lying so she'll go away and leave it all alone, or press somewhere else that isn't so tender. Then, after she presses and asks if it feels better, I feel like saying, "Yes, that's better," even before the muscle does release, just so she'll quit sooner. But I know that would not serve me well, and besides, there is no getting away from her. She can feel where the pain is.

Our whole relationship is really a matter of trust. Because I trust her expertise I feel the freedom and find the grace to stay with it. And through the persistence, I now have almost the full range of motion back in my ankle.

But it's a very vulnerable feeling to lie naked at someone else's hands and trust your body to his or her care. One day she was working with my lower back on a muscle I've strained swimming, and I could only respond "You've got to be kidding!" when she explained the stretch I need to do to work it back out. I felt like a pretzel.

But I trust her skill, judgment, and expertise. She has explained more to me about my body than a lifetime of doctors have. And I thought, as I drove away, "Does God know any less about our needs than this kind of human helper? Why do I so resist when God needs to exert 'ischemic pressure' to release my spiritual and psychological wounds?"

Just as we keep getting new muscle strains and kinks, so we continue to get new relationship strains and kinks. We will always be co-dependent, from the womb to death. That is the nature of the human condition—we used to call it "original sin"—and that is probably why Jesus urges us to "pray always."

To know this about ourselves is only depressing and discouraging if we were under the illusion that we have to fill in our missing pieces. The glory of the Christian faith is our belief that God is our missing piece.

Somehow, if we can begin to trust that God knows and cares for our deepest needs, at least as much as our massage therapists, we are then more able to endure the wait when that for which we pray seems slow in coming.

When we open to true prayer, we begin to see the bigger picture, beyond ourselves and our own narrow interests and desires. In 1989, when the telecast of the World Series was interrupted by the earthquake in San Francisco, the newscaster said, "The events here are much bigger than the World Series." That got my attention: I wondered if anything in America could be bigger than the World Series. At the time a sports columnist wrote, "Bury the World Series. Forget it. In the name of all of those who lie beneath huge slabs of concrete on I-880 in Oakland, California, in the name of those they pulled out from beneath the bricks and rubble of San Francisco's marina district, it ought to be done and over with. This is no time for playing baseball . . . for acting as if this part of the world is normal. Baseball should recognize this, but it doesn't." Earthquakes and hurricanes have a way of calling us back to take a serious look at our priorities in life. We realize that there is more than just our own agenda going on in the world.

The comedy *The Wonder Years,* on television that same evening, was about two friends in middle school. Paul, a Jewish boy, was inviting Kevin, the show's star, to his bar mitzvah, which was scheduled for the same day as Kevin's own thirteenth birthday party. Paul was disappointed that Kevin wasn't going to come to his bar mitzvah. Kevin said, "Paul, I'm sorry to tell you this, but you're not the center of the whole stupid world."

When the day of the bar mitzvah came, however, Kevin somehow realized that neither was he the center of the "whole stupid world." He put on a suit, went to the bar mitzvah, and apologized for being late. Paul's face lit up as Kevin entered the synagogue in the middle of the service. Kevin didn't understand one word of the worship celebration, of course, but he later recalled, "I slow-danced with Paul's Aunt Selma and ate too much . . . and when I look back on it, I sort of feel like it was my bar mitzvah, too!" And so it was.

In true prayer we get a sense that there are other agendas in the world besides our own. That doesn't mean we're worms and that our agenda is not important (which is one assumption we have often made, in our co-dependency), but it does mean that the kind of grandiosity that puts us and our agenda at the center of the universe (which is the other extreme we go to in our co-dependency)—that kind of grandiosity has to go. If nothing else, earthquakes and hurricanes call us back to that reality.

Abraham Heschel, a Jewish writer on prayer, says, "This is the task: in the darkest night to be certain of the dawn, certain of the power to turn a curse into a blessing, agony into a song . . . to go through hell and to continue to trust in the goodness of God. This is the challenge of the Way."[11]

Our job in life, then, becomes quite simple, though not easy. We are to pray always, and not lose heart.

Suggestions for Prayer or Journaling:

1. Read Shel Silverstein's *The Missing Piece* (New York: Harper and Row, 1976).

2. Where in your life is God applying "ischemic pressure" to heal your spiritual and psychological wounds?

3. Schedule an appointment for a massage with a retreat center which offers this as ministry.

STEP 12

Having had a spiritual awakening as the result of these steps, we try to carry this message to others, and to practice these principles in all our affairs.

Even As We Have Been Fully Understood

Read and reflect: 1 Corinthians 13:1-13

When I first came back into the institutional church, I wanted to reclaim my Christian roots. I looked through the Bible to find a starting place for my theology. I wanted to find at least one passage that I could already agree with and believe. This passage from 1 Corinthians was one of two passages I found. I concluded, with Paul, that love was where life is "at" and decided that love would be my main "centering principle" as a Christian.

The problem was that, in not having any training or education in how to interpret the scriptures, I came at this passage from my co-dependent "filter" through which I see and hear everything. Consequently the text became one more guilt trip which served to *block* my spiritual growth instead of *facilitating* it. What I heard in this passage was one more thing in life—love—that I couldn't get "right." I read the words and thought: "O God, I'm not patient," "O God, I do get irritable," "O God, I do get resentful." The litany of all the things I am (or am not) gets pretty long!

I was in a real bind, then, because I hadn't changed my mind about the importance of love as the center of the Christian life. I wondered, "If I am a Christian, then why can't I love?" That dilemma is probably what motivated me to go to seminary. I figured that seminary is where they taught about such dilemmas. This is what I've come to understand about it all.

First of all, we can't give out what we don't have. So we must begin by learning how to receive. In his book *Stage II Relationships,* Earnie Larsen says:

> The first thing God asks of us is to accept that we are loved. When we can accept that, we have the opportunity to be-

143

come all that we can be. If we can accept love, we can give love—the essential ingredient of a healthy relationship with another person. As one pole in our relationship, we need to develop the maturity and strength necessary to take care of ourselves, since we can only give to our relationships what we have and who we are.[1]

So there are two important and necessary things that need to happen before we can be loving. We need to accept God's love, and we need to love ourselves. One way to get a sense of God's love for us is to flip this passage around where it's describing what love is. Instead of hearing it describing what we would be like if we were loving, we need to hear it as describing what God is like since God is love.

God is patient and kind; God is not irritable or resentful; God does not rejoice at wrong; God bears all things; God endures all things.

That is to say, God, by nature, puts up with a lot. That is very freeing to me.

Until we can at least begin to understand the depth of love and patience God has for us, love coming in to us, and allow ourselves to receive that love from God through others, we will experience what some spiritual writers call a "deprivation neurosis," that is, an empty cup.

Love operates, then, not as an abstraction "out there" somewhere, but in the particulars of our real relationships, and it begins with love of ourselves. When Jesus tells us to love our neighbor as ourselves, there is a presumption there, and it is that all giving of love starts with love of self. John Bradshaw, in his book *Healing the Shame That Binds You,*[2] says, "Choosing to love ourselves is possible even if we have negative feelings about ourselves." Love is not a fuzzy feeling but a decision we make. "If we make the decision to love ourselves unconditionally, we will start feeling differently about ourselves." Bradshaw goes on to say that if we decide to love ourselves, we will be willing to give ourselves time and attention. He talks about the difference between being "human beings" and "human doings." If we are human doings, we drive ourselves and need more and more achievement in order to feel okay about ourselves.

If, however, we're willing to love and accept ourselves unconditionally, we will allow ourselves time to just be. We will set aside times when there's nothing we have to do and nowhere we have to go. We will allow ourselves solitude, a time of emotional and spiritual nourishment. We will take time for exercise, and for fun and entertainment. We will take vacations. We will learn to listen to ourselves by monitoring our feelings, needs and wants.

The work of paying attention to ourselves requires discipline, and discipline has been part and parcel of the life of prayer since the earliest times. In the early years of church history, groups of people met weekly to "inquire how their souls prosper." In the Twelve Step program, we call these meetings "recovery" groups or support groups, but it's the same thing by any name. That is why, when I experienced what goes on at ACOA meetings, I was motivated to ask the bishop about starting a Twelve Step ministry. What goes on at Twelve Step meetings really is church. Such groups provide honest feedback about where we are in the journey so we can move on in that journey.

Bradshaw says that "discipline demands telling the truth and being responsible for our own lives. If we love ourselves, we will live in reality."[3] Truth-telling and being responsible increase our self-esteem.

Assertiveness, which is based on self-love and self-valuing, is one of the most important ways, paradoxically, to become more loving, because it helps us to be real and truthful about our needs. When our needs are not met, we get hurt; and when we get hurt, we get angry; and when we get angry, we get even. So assertiveness, ironically, becomes a way of love for others. To receive is as important as to give in this love business. Thomas Merton explains how that is in this quote from one of his works:

> In the mystery of social love, there is found the realization of "the other," not only as one to be loved by us, so that we may perfect ourselves, but also as one who can become more perfect by loving us. The vocation to charity is a call not only to love but to be loved. The man or woman who does not care at all whether or not he or she is loved is ultimately unconcerned about the true welfare of the other and of society. Hence we cannot love unless we also consent to be loved in return.

So, knowing what we need becomes a crucial part of the life of love.

Maybe what we need is not more work but more time off. . . . Sometimes what we really need is not to be a pillar of iron but to surrender ourselves and allow our weakness and vulnerability to show through. Maybe what we need is to let others take care of us for a change. . . . The point is that if we are not in touch with our needs, or willing to get in touch with them, we cannot ask another person to be present to us. If we don't talk straight about our needs, chances are they will never be met, and if they're not, the result will be anger, which always leads to attempts to get even.[4]

Getting in touch with needs and feelings is no small agenda, especially for people who recognize themselves as co-dependents. A program for getting at our needs is essential if we are to build and improve relationships with others. It takes a great deal of energy to function in healthy relationships, and that energy is blocked when we're using it all up sitting on repressed memories that we're trying to keep from surfacing. As a friend described it to me, it's like trying to hold a beach ball under water; it just keeps bobbing up somewhere else.

Love, then, is not what we first thought. It begins at home, "in here," and once it's rooted and grounded "in here," it won't manifest "out there" in the counterfeit shape of "people pleasing." Jesus is our model par excellence of the fact that love means confronting people when we see them on a path of self-destruction. Some of the most loving decisions I have made were decisions not to marry people who came "church shopping" for a place to have their wedding. I have authority to perform weddings, but it may be more loving *not* to do so.

Jesus always got below the level of what was *allowed* in order to look more closely at what was *real*, to discover what would be love in any situation. To love is not the same as to be *thought of* or *seen as* loving. Our motives need to be considered, and often what looks like love is self-motivated, the desire to be doing something that makes us look loving, and what looks like rejection is actually love.

Love is not a fuzzy feeling, but a decision, and once we decide to love, then there are skills to learn that most of us were never taught. Lacking these skills does not make us bad or evil, but it does make relationships difficult. Love is never something we do in the abstract; we don't love "humankind." Love is not something we ever do outside of relationships. If learning to love is Paul's and Christ's message to us, and if love exists only in relationships, then at the core of recovery, and of the Christian life, is becoming a person increasingly capable of functioning in healthy relationships. Co-dependency, by definition, is those self-defeating behaviors we have learned that diminish our capacity to initiate or participate in loving relationships. We have difficulty participating in loving healthy relationships because we lack precisely the skills and traits needed. The good news is that those skills can be learned.

One of the skills needed is communication, and effective communication is one of the most important ingredients in relationship building. It is the foundation of trust, and without trust there can be no relationship. When we have no way to talk with each other, to understand each other, to understand God, or to sense God's acceptance of us, we are unable to love because we don't experience love coming in. One of the most powerful experiences of love I received during the first year of my Twelve Step ministry was when a man from the traditional church came into my office and asked to borrow my copy of the issue of *Newsweek* in which the cover story was about ACOAs. His visit was like receiving a big greeting card that said, "Hi! I care about you and your ministry!"

It is equally important to communicate our concerns to each other. Doing that clearly and directly is also love, and it puts the concern where it belongs and can be dealt with. The single most common reason for failed relationships is not talking straight, not telling each other how we really feel, how something is affecting us, and therefore what we need. I believe, with John Bradshaw, that underneath every failed relationship, every crime of violence, every act of terror, at the center of every broken family, there is a deep ache that was never heard—often never spoken—and maybe never even allowed to be felt . . . never validated as really being there. The violence gets acted out externally while the real violence is always going on within.

We don't understand the reasons for hijacking a plane, for dumping a person out on the runway, for placing a newborn baby in a trash dumpster, for raping a classmate. God alone understands.

We too are fully understood by God alone. Truly we see now in a mirror dimly. Now we know only in part. One day we shall understand fully, even as we have been fully understood.

Suggestions for Prayer or Journaling:

1. Reread 1 Corinthians 13 and substitute the word "God" for "love" wherever it appears. Journal your feelings that arise out of this experience.

2. Set aside five minutes today, when there is nothing you have to do and no place you have to go, to simply sit and be with yourself. Increase it to ten minutes the second day, fifteen the third, and so on to find your "minimum daily requirement" of solitude. Give this now as a gift to yourself on an ongoing basis.

3. Write down three needs that you have which are not being met and which you are not asserting. Write a plan of action to get them met.

4. What is one situation in your life where "tough love" is now required of you?

5. Read The Song of Songs as a poem of love in which God addresses you.

An Abandon That Will Be Despised

Read and reflect: John 12:1-8

When we read the scriptures, one of the issues we have to confront right off the bat is the tendency most of us have toward "all-or-nothing" thinking. In this passage, for example, we need to deal with the apparent contradiction between Jesus' general teaching about giving to the poor and his statement here that "the poor you always have with you." The tendency for co-dependents is to read into that statement ". . . so don't worry about them," and that is the kind of either/or thinking that gets us into trouble more generally in life, not just in reading the Bible.

What is being said here is not that Jesus is changing his mind about the needs of the poor, but that he is aware of his own need to receive this ministry from Mary right now. He knows he is headed for the cross, and Mary, at an unconscious level, realizes that too, and she is anointing him for burial. There are several important things to learn from this passage.

First of all (staying for a moment with the issue of all-or-nothing thinking), we have in this passage the same Mary and Martha who, back in an earlier story, were giving Jesus hospitality, each in her own way. Recall how Martha, who was scurrying around working in the kitchen, became resentful of Mary's way, which was to sit quietly at Jesus' feet in contemplative adoration, listening to him. Martha thinks Mary should be doing her share of the busy work, but Jesus tells them in that story that only one thing is really necessary in life, and what Mary is doing is just as important as what Martha is doing. That is, the one necessary thing is loving the Lord, sitting at Christ's feet, so to speak. It's not "either/or," it's both/and. We love God both in action and in contemplation.

So here we have Mary again, sitting at Jesus' feet and moved, out of her prior spiritual awakening, to love him in an extravagant way, not only by anointing his feet with this expensive oil, which would have been worth about eleven months' wages, but by drying his feet with her hair. In biblical times, in Palestine, no respectable woman would unbind her hair in public; that was a sign of immorality. But here, Mary never even thought of that in her abandon to take a chance, to dare to offer a degree of love and care that would be despised and misunderstood by people there. Judas just couldn't understand that kind of abandon, that someone would or could offer a depth of love like that. But it's a love which is really always there for us if we appropriate it. That is, Mary was actually imparting God's love to Jesus in that act.

Jesus understood and was able to receive the gift for what it was. And when I first seriously pondered the meaning of this passage some years back, I found myself wondering then: Is it only in Jesus' divinity that he was able to receive Mary's gift? Do we need Jesus' own level of sanctity or holiness in our lives before we too can recognize these kinds of gifts coming our way? Or could it be that even we, placed here as we are in our humanity, in the "not-yet-ness" of our everyday lives, struggling as we are "in-process"—could it be that even we, placed here in our humanity, could somehow be so "divinized" that we might also recognize this depth of love that's really there, freely offered to us?

I think it's only as we do receive that we are able then—strengthened and empowered—to abandon, take the chance of being misunderstood and despised, and to give that degree of care to others in our midst. Again, giving and receiving go together. It's not an either/or. Jesus knew that, and that is why, on this occasion before his own journey to the cross, he tells Judas, "Let her alone." In the other gospel accounts of this story, Jesus adds, "Truly, I say to you, wherever the gospel is preached in the whole world, what this woman has done will be told in memory of her."

But Judas could not understand love's extravagance. His gift for handling money became more important to him than love, so that God's purpose for his life got set aside.

What we see in Judas—and not just Judas, for he is simply a metaphor for any of us whose view of reality gets warped—what we see in Judas is how our view of people and events can become warped if we begin to look at life through distorted filters . . . filters which color reality falsely and prevent us from seeing things as they really are.

In Florida one year, the director of the retreat house where I stayed let me borrow a really good book to read. But she needed it back by the next day to prepare for a retreat she was leading around it, so I had only this one day to read it before I left.

On the way to the beach I remembered that I now have bifocals, and with my old sunglasses I wouldn't be able to read, so I stopped to buy a pair of sunglasses, the kind that clip on. The only color they had was this weird yellow, and since I didn't want to waste the morning shopping for sunglasses, I just went ahead and bought them so I could get on my way. As I drove, the "filter" these glasses created by their yellow color altered the world outside so radically that I could only tell that a small lake which I passed was water by the ripples in the surface, not by the color. It was weird, but since I could see to drive, it was OK, and I drove on to the island. There on the beach, I noticed that my lavender, aqua, and purple swim suit became, with my sunglasses on, a kind of psychedelic or fluorescent orange, green and burgundy. At first I could just smile and separate "reality" from my filter, but as the hours wore on and I kept seeing the suit peripherally as I was reading, I started feeling self-conscious sitting on the beach in this weird psychedelic suit that would be appropriate for someone in junior high school. At that point I put the book down and paid attention to what had happened in my mind, and what had happened was that my skewed perception of reality had *become* reality as I went on absorbed in the reading of the book, that is, without conscious attention to the filter I was wearing. I looked out at all the people walking on the beach in their yellow hats and yellow suits, and weird chartreuses and pinks, and "forgot" that those colors were not *their* colors, but *my* colors.

I think that is largely what has happened to us as co-dependents. Our view of the world depends on the filter through which we see it, and memories, when they are not used to move us forward in our thinking, can become hindrances as we anticipate the action of our God in the future. Isaiah reminds us to remain not anchored in the past, but to behold the new thing God is doing. "Now it springs forth," he says, "and do you not perceive it?"

Sometimes, if we discover we have been looking at the world through an old filter that is greatly distorting reality, we may want to make some changes. Changes are never without a price, but the filter which may have served us well at the time—and even have been necessary to accomplish an earlier purpose—may now be destructive to our current purpose. In the example I've used, the sunglasses I bought were seven dollars, but it was not a total waste of money, for reading the book that day has become the springboard for some teaching I will now do. Yet, for the long run, those yellow sunglasses have to go, and it will cost me at least another seven dollars, and probably more like three hundred dollars eventually, for what will serve me best and longest. But it's always a choice I can make, whether to spend the money at all and how much to spend.

The choice in today's gospel lesson was the same, really. "Both [of Jesus'] disciples [Mary and Judas] were in the presence of the Light of the World. One recognized the moment, the other sank back into darkness."⁵ The choice is ours. Do we want to see reality clearly? Are we willing to pay the price to follow the way, the truth, and the life? It will cost more than thirty pieces of silver, but the cross that it leads to is much preferable to suicide, which was Judas' ultimate choice.

So, Jesus' forthcoming death means two different things to two different people. Mary has a vision that sees and appreciates Jesus' transcendent identity, and her act of anointing his feet "foreshadows not only Jesus' own washing of his disciples' feet but also the supreme irony of the triumph of the cross."⁶ She sees through a different "filter." She understands this kind of abandon.

"Which of our values need to be challenged this Lent? What in our lives needs to be turned upside down so that God can set things right? In this gospel text, we have a topsy-turvy upheaval of the world's values. Judas sees only the value of the ointment but not the value of persons, specifically the person of Jesus, on whom the ointment is poured."⁷

Do we see our own value? Are you "worth" having eleven months' salary poured over your feet? If you want a reality check on that, think back to how you reacted internally the last time you read that there would be a footwashing service during Holy Week. Did you make a mental note to come that night and receive, to be anointed and nurtured? Or did you think to yourself, "Gross"? Our answer may reveal to us what value we're placing on ourselves.

The first time I ever heard of "footwashing" my reaction was,

"Gross!" That was about nine years ago when I was serving on a Cursillo team, and the footwashing service was to be part of our renewal weekend. But when I actually experienced having another gently dry my feet with a towel—no one on the weekend was as free as Mary to use one's hair!—it was a real blessing, a depth of love that, actually, is always there, God's blessing, God's own undying love.

Some Holy Week, abandon your self-preoccupation, take the chance, and dare to give and receive that kind of care. It is an abandon that the world despises and cannot understand. But in this abandon is our divinity, that we are able to receive, and somehow recognize, the depth of love that's really there for us. Abandon, take the chance and dare!

MASTER OF DIVINITY

Why is it that, when Mary dried
your Son's feet with her hair,
no one but he could recognize
this gift from you she shared—
abandon that would be despised,
misunderstood by people there?
No one would take the chance and dare
to offer that degree of care . . .
a depth of Love that's always there,
a mystic blessing from above,
the mystery of undying love.

Is it in his divinity
that he was able to receive,
or could it be that even we,
placed here in our humanity,
could somehow be so divinized
that we might also recognize
this depth of Love that's really there,
abandon, take the chance and dare
give and receive that kind of care—
a mystic blessing from above,
the mystery of undying Love.

Suggestions for Prayer or Journaling:

1. Through what "filter" do you look at life? Is it a filter which, long ago, served a useful purpose toward survival in a dysfunctional environment, but which now is simply making things "weird" and distorted? Journal your sense of what's going on now that may skew your perceptions of reality.

2. Speak to God in prayer about what you expect the cost to be to change filters. Listen for the response. Write what you hear.

ALL TWELVE STEPS

Why Suffering?

Read and reflect: 2 Corinthians 1:1–11

One hot day in August 1981 I was having lunch with a man who had been the spiritual director on a renewal weekend I'd made a couple of years before, and who was now to be one of my references for my application to seminary. He was on the faculty of the seminary to which I was applying, and so he seemed like the logical person to now serve as a reference. We had made this luncheon date to sort of "catch up" with each other's lives. I was sharing the ways I was experiencing God moving in my life, and telling him that I had so many questions, things I wanted to know and learn, and that was why I was enrolling in seminary. My assumption was that somewhere "they" had it all figured out, and my job was simply to go and read the right books, or listen to the right people, and find out the answers. I figured he was probably one of those "right" people.

I said, at one point, "I want to understand about pain and evil and suffering, and why God allows that, and where 'salvation' is in all *that!*" He stirred his tea gently and thoughtfully and reverently as he began to answer very quietly, and I thought, "Here it comes! I'm about to find out the secret of pain and suffering right here at Willard's restaurant!" And he put his spoon down and looked me carefully in the eye and said, slowly, "You'll struggle with that for a long time." And that turns out to be a word for all of us.

To a large extent we *can* understand and explain suffering. Not only that, but we even *choose* it because of our misplaced priorities —if not individually, then collectively. We prioritize our values in America. If the money that currently goes for athletes' salaries— just the excess over, say, a figure of $150,000 each—were put into cancer research, we would have an entirely different medical reality in this country. That's one observation we can make from last year's flap over major league baseball. We choose sports over health in this country. And so we pay the price.

Likewise, we collectively choose the highway death toll from drunk drivers. We generally don't write our lawmakers until our loved one is killed. If we really loved our neighbor as ourself, we'd be up in arms about that kind of highway slaughter before our loved one is hurt by it.

But there's more to suffering that we need to address. In the movie *Oh God, Book II*, Tracy is a little girl about eight years old who sees and talks with God, played by George Burns. Tracy runs away at one point because the adults are going to put her in an institution. Like Joan of Arc, she refuses to back down on her claim to have talked with God. While Tracy is sitting in the train station, God comes to take her home. As they're walking out of the station, Tracy initiates this dialogue with God around the problem of suffering:

"Can I ask you a question?"

"Go ahead," God replies.

"Why do you let bad things happen?"

"You ask very good questions. You know, Tracy, things that you might think are bad are not always bad. Sometimes there's a purpose you're not aware of."

"But what about sickness? What about kids my age who get sick and die? Those are really bad things, aren't they?"

"Those are bad things—yes, pain and suffering! That's a hard one to explain!"

"I'll bet!" Tracy says sarcastically.

"I know this sounds like a copout," replies God, "but there's nothing I can really do about pain and suffering. It's built into the system."

"Which you invented!" Tracy replies angrily.

"Right, but my problem was, I never could figure out how to make anything with just one side to it. You ever see a front without a back?"

"No."

"Top without a bottom?"

"No."

"Up without a down?"

"No."

"Okay! Then there can't be good without bad, life without death, pleasure without pain—that's how it is. If I take sad away, happy has to go with it. If anyone knows another way, I wish they'd put it in the suggestion box!"

Tracy says, wistfully, "I guess some day I'll understand."

"You do, you'll be the first," says God. "Some things can't be grasped. What's the end? The end of time? The end of the universe? Even Einstein flunked that one!"

That dialogue is a better explanation than I've ever heard or read in any theology book about why there is suffering. Partly, it just goes hand in hand with our being given freedom of choice—as in the issue of the sports vs. health priorities. However, the question of what purpose suffering serves is left unanswered.

If Jesus suffered in order to work our "salvation," and we are to "follow him," then it must be that somehow in our suffering we will be participants in the salvation of others. We will be "little Christs," which is what "Christian" really means. A symbol that is particularly meaningful to me is the symbol some United Methodist churches use for a logo: a cross whose upper portion is shaped in the form of a shepherd's crook. It speaks to me because, for me, the only real "shepherding" is only and always in "suffering with." Here are some real-life examples of where that has been precisely the way I've seen it work.

When Aaron, our seven year old, was born, he inhaled some fluid from the sac during the C-section before they could get him out, and he got aspiration pneumonia, which developed quickly into hyaline membrane disease, and so he went directly into the neonatal intensive care unit, on oxygen.

For whatever reason, none of those who were "supposed" to minister to one in such situations could touch me with their words. A pastor came and read the 23rd Psalm but this didn't feel like a green pasture, and I *was* afraid of the shadow of death. The nurses were very task-oriented, and had no idea of the added pain it caused when they brought my roommates' babies in and explained how to nurse them. I didn't want anybody to give me false assurances; I just wanted some honest acknowledgement of whatever was going on. I would have been OK if someone had even said, "I see your baby's going down the tubes." At least that would have validated my perception of reality and my feelings of helplessness around it.

One evening I was in the neonatal intensive care unit tending to Aaron when I looked up to see a friend of ours, standing at the window, wiping a tear from her eyes. That non-verbal gesture was sacramental for me: an outward and visible sign of an inward invisible grace, because in it I experienced God's tears, God's love and care for us at this time. I knew then that someone understood how this felt.

What I only later got in touch with was how she got to be a person of compassion for me. She married a man whose first wife had died in pregnancy, and that baby had been lost as well. When she came into that family, she picked up the pieces of the two older boys' frustration and hurt and anger, and she discovered what a problem-pregnancy and the death of a child can do to a family. The three year old was spitting on other kids in the neighborhood, and the pre-school asked if she would come down and physically hold him on her lap during story time. The tears she cried that night were partly a remembering of her pain and their suffering from their own earlier experience. But God used those tears and the earlier pain and suffering to bring grace and love to me. I've concluded that's really pretty much how suffering seems to work to God's purposes.

Here's another story that, to me, is symbolic of the larger "salvation" message: The summer I did my Clinical Pastoral Education at the psychiatric unit of a hospital, the floor to which I was assigned housed the "special care unit" where people were brought from other wings if they were a danger to themselves or others. It was a cluster of rooms with only a mattress on the floor, or a bed, so the patients couldn't hurt themselves by throwing furniture; and whenever anyone was brought into this unit, it was like a tornado alert. All the hallways were closed off, doors were shut, and wherever you were, and whatever you were doing, you were to stay put. I was frightened to death of the whole unit, and spent the first seven weeks feeling guilty that I didn't have whatever it took to be able to go and work with any of the people there. I just avoided the whole section. One thing about CPE is they let you learn at your own pace, and you can choose what you're ready for and when. A classmate of mine had been decked by a woman at another psych hospital and I decided right off that I wasn't that committed to helping these people. But I felt badly about that.

One night, I dreamed there was a black block, about sixteen inches thick, labeled "faith" that was propping open the door to the special care unit, just wide enough for me to get in and back out. I decided God was calling me to trust and to go in and do this. The next day we had a seventeen year old girl brought in.

I asked the attendant to see if the girl would like to see a chaplain, and the girl said, "OK." I pulled up a chair by her bed and sat down next to her, where she was restrained and lying spread-eagle on the bed.

I introduced myself as the chaplain assigned to that unit, and said that if there were any way I could help at all to make God present to her, I would like to do that—whether by listening, talking or whatever. I really didn't know what she needed, and had no idea what to say. She said, plaintively, "I just want to get *out* of here!" I then looked at her—really *looked* at her, for the first time: the pink straitjacket around her chest, the two-inch leather straps around her wrists and ankles, and all at once I got in touch with all my own restraints—the leather bindings I keep on myself, and that I had, in fact, been wearing on this very job for seven weeks. My fears had kept me restrained from all that I could have been. Tears came down my cheeks as I identified with what it's like to be bound and tied and unable to get yourself out of it. I really felt both our pain; and in response to her statement that she just wanted to get out of there, all I could say, with tears running down my own face now, was, "I guess you *do*."

But then an interesting thing happened. It was all non-verbal, and it's hard to describe. She had had a kind of hurt-dog expression on her face the whole time of our visit, but when she saw my tears, her expression changed to something I can't exactly describe—surprise, I guess. It was as if no one in her whole life had ever cared about her, and she was now experiencing that. The fact is that my tears were as much for me as for her, but I think we both realized at that point that those are God's tears we cry for each other in this life. She relaxed then, and went to sleep.

The way you get out of the special care unit is by calming down so that you are no longer a danger to yourself or others. And so, having now relaxed, she was then allowed, when she woke, to return to the adolescent unit. This is how "salvation" works: through suffering—our vicarious suffering for one another, in the same way that Jesus suffered for us. That is why the Good Shepherd logo and cross have such meaning to me. It is a very simple design with a whole lot of theology behind it.

When someone comes to me who is suicidal, I would not be able to help if I had not known how it feels to experience despair; I would have no understanding of the depths to which the human soul can sink. The person would only be my "project." One can only know how that feels—how powerless, how helpless, not to be able to get out of it yourself, even as much as you want to, if one has been there. Faith is a gift of God and not a work of ours. It is not something you can drum up. It comes to us as in my dream of the black block: unbidden in the night, when we least expect it. When people try to be helpful by sending cards that say "Have faith!" or "Buck up!" that only makes us feel worse, because we can't.

Ernst Kasemann, a New Testament writer, says that the good news is, first of all, that God is love: "For a God who is incapable of suffering is a being who cannot be involved. Suffering and injustice do not affect him. And because he is so completely insensitive, he cannot weep, for he has no tears. But the one who cannot suffer cannot love either. So he is also a loveless being."

God's "perfection" is in God's compassion. So we are to be compassionate as God is compassionate, and the way that gets worked in us is through suffering. Not the suffering that God "puts on us," as you will hear some people believe, when they attribute their suffering to "God's will," but simply the suffering that is part of the human condition. Why does a baby suck in air that turns out to be fluid instead? Because the baby hasn't had much experience at being born yet!

When you look up "suffering" and "perfection" in a concordance, you find them occurring together in the same passages in five different places in scripture. They go together. As George Burns said, "There's no top without a bottom, no front without a back, no up without a down." When the teacher says that Johnny is home with chicken pox today, the moment of empathy and compassion for Johnny comes out of your own chicken pox experience. That moment becomes prayer. This is what it means that prayer, ultimately, is not something we say, but what we are. The pray-er *becomes* prayer.

The other thing you discover when you look up "suffering" in the concordance is that it is tied together with growth in faith. 1 Peter says:

It may now be necessary for you to be sad for a while because of the many kinds of trials you suffer. Their purpose is to prove that your faith is genuine. Even gold, which can be destroyed, is tested by fire; and so your faith, which is much more precious than gold, must also be tested, so that it may endure (1 Pet 1:6–9).

On the day I started seminary, I thought my faith had already been tested. I had undergone CAT scans and EEG's to rule out a brain tumor, and since I had had to work through the possibility of leaving my young family, I thought I had now passed the test and was "home free." I thought the fear of death was the "biggie" you had to get past. But it was in seminary that I discovered that the headaches were due to thirty-seven years of repressed anger, and that working through that can be harder than dying! I would never have chosen what was to come in the next several years as I got in touch with memories that were very painful. But when I look back now, I see how suffering has made me grow up a lot. My faith then was not in God, but in my faith.

That is the kind of dross that has to keep being burned off in the fire before any of us is ready for authentic ministry to others. Only now do I understand that faith is a journey, and none of us ever "arrives" in this lifetime. Nor did Abraham and Moses. Faith development is a process in which our individual torches periodically feel as if they are flickering and in danger of going out. The good news is that the true Light does not go out.

So, the question is not whether we will suffer, but whether we will suffer for the right reasons. A woman once told me that her husband, when he is angry with her, yells, in front of their preschooler, "I hope you rot in hell!" Toleration of that kind of abuse is not the kind of suffering Jesus had in mind for us. It is masochism and comes out of low self-esteem.

Peter has some helpful words to us about suffering for the right reasons:

Beloved, do not be surprised at the fiery ordeal that comes upon you, as though something strange were happening to you. But rejoice insofar as you share Christ's sufferings, that you may also rejoice and be glad when his glory is revealed. But let none of you suffer as a murderer or a thief or a meddler in other people's affairs. . . . Cast all your anxieties on God, for God cares about you. Be sober and watchful. Resist the evil one, firm in your faith, knowing that the same experience of suffering is required of your sisters and brothers throughout the world. And after you have suffered a little while, the God of all grace, who has called you to share eternal glory in union with Christ, will restore, establish, and strengthen you. To God be the dominion for ever and ever (1 Pet 4:12–15; 5:7–11).

Suggestions for Prayer or Journaling:

1. Where in your life has suffering helped you grow up? What would you change about your experiences of suffering?

2. Draw your own shepherd's crook and reflect on the ways people in your life have "shepherded" you through their suffering with you.

That They May Have Life

Read and reflect: John 10:1–10; Acts 2:42–47

These scriptures are very powerful for me, because I see in them the essence of the Christian life. The words speak of God's faithfulness to us as a shepherd cares for the sheep. It becomes clear that out of that care, the ability is generated within us to care for each other. We bask in this care, then, day by day, attending temple together, breaking bread in our homes, partaking of food with glad and generous hearts, such that we can share and give of ourselves and our possessions—all because we recognize Jesus in the breaking of the bread. This is the life of prayer.

We notice that the sheep hear the voice of the shepherd who calls them by name and leads them out. It is in the discovering of our real and true identity—the being called by name—that we are empowered to move out to others. Then, as we go out, we are protected like sheep. We are not protected *from* service; we are protected *in* service.

I got a call as I was pondering these texts from another United Methodist pastor who wanted to preach about the nature of Christian service and where the line is drawn between Christian caring and co-dependence. I told him to come over and we would struggle with that together. When we got together, I shared with him my belief that one of the most destructive things in Christian life and teaching is the idea of service as obligation. When we begin to look at service as some kind of duty, I think it is precisely there that we go astray.

Timmen Cermak, in his book *Diagnosing and Treating Co-dependence,* suggests three ways to distinguish what he calls "co-ing" from authentic service or helping others. Two of the suggestions have to do with the relationship of the action to one's personal needs, and to one's personal autonomy. Cermak suggests that we ask ourselves whether we are acting out of a sense of obligation, which generally is a cause for resentment and rarely feels like "abundant life." He uses the example of the parent who leaves work early and skips an important meeting to attend a child's Little League game, and he suggests that if the parent secretly resents having missed the meeting, then attending the game is not the generous and loving act it seems. Pretending that something is a simple act and there will be no repercussions from having ignored one's own needs represents "co-ing."

As to one's sense of personal autonomy, Cermak says that when we feel bound to be kind in order to keep others happy and avoid the risk of being abandoned, it is likely also that we are "co-ing." The order is out of order. Sacrifices, to be true self-giving sacrifices, are never in-order-to, but always out-of-the-fullness-of.

Jesus came that we might have life and have it abundantly. "Abundant life—rich, plentiful, ample—is an invitation for full and responsible life now, and in the pasture of God's graciousness, we will be empowered for such life."[1] One thing I've figured out is that to have a real sense of what abundant life is, we have to look beyond what we expect that to be. It isn't life without conflict, life with no confusions, life with no misunderstandings.

I think it has more to do with becoming attentive to the ways in which the very conflict and confusions and misunderstandings of life become "avenues for awakening within us the recognition of the divine. . . . Becoming attentive to the signs of life and love around us, searching for the real, results in an integrated lifestyle that empowers us and frees us and those with whom we come in contact. The consequence is the inbreaking of the realm and reign of God that bears the fruit of abundant life for all who graze in its pastures."[2]

Prior to my ordination, I was interviewed by a six-member board of elders about the work of our Twelve Step church. One man on this team had a difficult time understanding what I do. I was having an even more difficult time trying to clarify that the Twelve Steps are not a narrow one-dimensional focus, as he thought, but a very wide focus which encompasses the whole Christian tradition.

I had just shared earlier in my ministry evaluation session for this interview that my biggest frustration in this ministry is when people "outside" think what I do in the Twelve Step church is so "weird," when what I'm doing is really no different from what I did in my internship church up the street, except that now I include the language of the Twelve Steps in things. So, I kept trying to explain that what we call the Fifth Step, for instance, is what the church knows as "confession of sin," and once you can make the translations, this ministry is not all that "weird" or unusual.

The interviewer kept coming back again to the question of how I will deal someday in a rural appointment with a farm family who doesn't know the Twelve Steps. (Later some of my parishioners assured me that farm families *will* be familiar with the Twelve Steps, but that's hindsight!) Finally, I said in exasperation, "I feel like I'm not getting through to you." He said, "You just did." Something had finally clicked and he understood at last.

Later in the interview they asked me, "What is eternal life?" I said, "What just happened here this last hour is eternal life. I felt so unable to be understood, so misperceived, which is always alienating, and then, at once, we were together here. That is eternal life!" And I believe that. Eternal life happens despite the conflict, in the midst of conflict, even out of our frustration.

> Abundant life means that we struggle for justice and freedom, compassion and laughter, hope and intimacy, for ourselves and all persons. It is living in trust and power that God's spirit will strengthen us to face the demands of living our values for the sake of values, whatever the cost.[3]

> It is not enough to have life . . . we must live life, feel it, open up to it, let it sway us and have its way with us. Life's real enemy is not pain, not even death; life's enemy is boredom.[4]

We need to look beyond, to see, "behind all of the darkness that assails us, the glow of God's love that affirms us. We need to look beyond ourselves toward the image of God's coming reign where we are truly one, in Jesus' name."[5]

The Good Shepherd calls us by name and leads us out. After bringing us out, the Shepherd goes before us and we follow. We are protected, not from service, but in service. This is abundant life.

Suggestions for Prayer or Journaling:

1. Reflect upon your current service in your church or Christian community. In what ways have you been acting out of a sense of

"Christian duty" and, down-deep, resenting it? Write out an inner wisdom dialogue with Jesus and voice your resentments. Listen for his voice, calling you by name, and hear his counsel to you at this time.

2. Reflect upon instances where you have made "sacrifices" that, at the time, seemed altruistic but which now, upon careful examination, were actions taken to placate others or to avoid the risk of feeling abandoned by others. Journal your thoughts and feelings; then listen in the stillness for the Shepherd's voice.

Notes

STEP 1

1. Ole Hallesby, *Prayer* (Minneapolis: Augsburg, 1924) 30ff.
2. Maria Theresa Winter, *Preparing the Way of the Lord* (Nashville: Abingdon, 1978) 167.
3. *Homily Service* (Washington D.C.: The Liturgical Conference), December 1988, 14.
4. Ibid. 16.
5. Ibid. 14.

STEP 2

1. Fr. Leo Booth, "Spirituality for Adult Children: An Evening with Fr. Leo Booth," Tape 17, Program S 268, U.S. Journal Training, Inc., from the conference on *Children of Alcoholics,* Chattanooga, September 25–27, 1986.

STEP 3

1. Earnie Larsen and Carol Larsen Hegarty, *Days of Healing, Days of Joy* (Center City: Hazelden, 1987).
2. *Homiletics* (North Canton: Communication Resources, March, 1989) 3.
3. Ibid. 4.
4. Ibid. 5.
5. Wording from John Wesley's original covenant renewal service.
6. *The Book of Worship for Church and Home* (Nashville: United Methodist Publishing House, 1964).

7. *Alcoholics Anonymous* (New York: Alcoholics Anonymous World Services, 1939) 67.

STEP 4

1. Terry Kellogg, "Hidden Anger in Recovery," available from Terry Kellogg, 20300 Excelsior Blvd., Minneapolis, Minnesota 55331.

STEP 5

1. Carl Jung, *The Practice of Psychotherapy: Essays on the Psychology of the Transference and Other Subjects* (Princeton: Bollingen Series XX, 1954), Volume 16 of the Collected Works, 57.
2. Aldo Carotenuto, *Eros and Pathos: Shades of Love and Suffering* (Toronto: Inner City Books, 1989) 11–12.
3. Ibid. 18.

STEP 6

1. *The Twelve Steps—A Way Out* (San Diego: Recovery Publications, 1987) 71.
2. Ibid. 72.
3. *The Twelve Steps for Adult Children* (San Diego: Recovery Publications, 1987).
4. *Homily Service,* February 1989, 7, 9.
5. *Homiletics,* January-March 1989, 24.
6. *Homily Service,* February 1989, 10.
7. Ibid.
8. *The Cloud of Unknowing,* translated by Ira Progoff (New York: Dell Publishing, 1957, 1983).

STEP 7

1. *The Twelve Steps—A Way Out,* 78.
2. This section (six paragraphs) draws heavily upon commentary in *Homily Service,* August 1989, 43–45.
3. Ibid. 48–49.

STEP 8

1. *Homily Service,* May 1990, 12, 16.
2. Ibid. 13.
3. Stanza 6 of "Where Charity and Love Prevail," © World Library Publications, Inc. Reprinted by permission.

STEP 9

1. Peggy Moon, "Rhythms of Life," in *Weavings* (Nashville: The Upper Room, September/October 1987), 37.
2. Ibid. 38.
3. "Ferreting Truth," in *Spiritual Life* (Washington, D.C.: Province of the Discalced Carmelite Friars, Spring 1986) 20–23.
4. Exegetical material in this section drawn from lecture notes from Rev. Van Bogard Dunn.
5. *Stairway to Serenity: The Eleventh Step* (Center City: Hazelden Foundation, 1988) 71.

STEP 10

1. Carl Jung, *The Practice of Psychotherapy,* Collected Works, Vol. 16, 55.
2. Melody Beattie, "Beyond Codependency: Moving from Powerlessness to Personal Power," Tape #39, Program H 108, First National Conference on Codependency, Scottsdale, Arizona, September 6–9, 1989, U.S. Journal Training, Inc.
3. Ibid.

STEP 11

1. *Homily Service,* July 1989, 47.
2. Leonard W. Mann, *Where Two or Three are Gathered* (Lima: C.S.S. Publishing, 1986) 63.
3. "Come to the Water," John Foley, S.J. Copyright © 1978 by John B. Foley, S.J., and New Dawn Music.
4. Terry Kellogg, "Factors, Facets, Forces, and Faces of Sexual

Compulsivity," Tape #36, Program H 108, First National Conference on Codependency, Scottsdale, Arizona, September 6–9, 1989, U.S. Journal Training, Inc.

5. Alice Miller, *For Your Own Good: Hidden Cruelty in Child-Rearing and the Roots of Violence* (New York: Farrar, Miller, Straus, Giroux, 1983).

6. James Nelson, *The Intimate Connection: Male Sexuality, Masculine Spirituality* (Philadelphia: Westminster, 1988).

7. Ibid. 103.

8. Ibid. 102.

9. Ibid. 103.

10. Kellogg, "Factors, Facets, Forces, and Faces of Sexual Compulsivity."

11. Abraham Heschel, *A Passion for Truth* (New York: Farrar, Straus & Giroux, 1973) 301.

STEP 12

1. Earnie Larsen, *Stage II Relationships: Love Beyond Addiction* (San Francisco: Harper & Row, 1987) 114.

2. John Bradshaw, *Healing the Shame That Binds You* (Deerfield Beach: Health Communications, 1988) 158–161.

3. Ibid. 160.

4. Larsen, *Stage II Relationships,* 49–50.

5. *Homily Service,* March 1989, 17.

6. Ibid. 20.

7. Ibid.

ALL TWELVE STEPS

1. *Homily Service,* May 1990, 5.

2. Ibid. 6.

3. Ibid.

4. Walter Burghardt, quoted in *Homily Service,* May 1990, 8.

5. Adapted from Paul A. Laughlin's prayer of confession, printed in *Worship Aids for Year A,* Series II Lectionary Worship Aids, Cycle A (Lima: Ohio: C.S.S. Publishing, 1989) 118.